SCIENCE ON STAGE

ANTHOLOGY

EDITED BY
TESSA BRIDAL
AND SUSAN
MCCORMICK

ASSOCIATION OF SCIENCE–TECHNOLOGY CENTERS

© Association of Science-Technology Centers, April 1991

ISBN 0-944040-26-8

For more information, contact:
The Association of Science-Technology Centers
1025 Vermont Ave., NW, Suite 500
Washington, DC 20005-3516
202/783-7200

Printed on Recycled Paper

CONTENTS

Preface	5
Foreword	7
Center Stage in the Museum: Using Theater to Present the Issues	9
Alice in Numberland	15
Playwright's Notes	19
Production History and Notes	20
Production Rights	21
Script	22
George Washington Carver: Born to Succeed	37
Playwright's Notes	39
Production History and Notes	39
Production Rights	40
Script	40
Sara the Scientist	49
Production History and Notes	52
Production Rights	54
Script	55
Bibliography	70
The Soap Opera	71
Playwright's Notes	74
Production Notes	76
Production Rights	79
Script	79
Wondrous Visions: A Visit with Leonardo da Vinci	99
Playwright's Notes	101
Production History and Notes	102
Production Rights	106
Script	106
About ASTC	115

PREFACE

S*cience on Stage* is the first published anthology of plays written for and performed at science centers and museums. The plays presented here vary greatly in size of cast and production, but all share the goal of communicating aspects of science and technology through theater.

Theater provides an educational tool that complements those traditionally used at science centers. Plays are "live" in every sense, and compensate for the more impersonal nature of most exhibits. They are excellent vehicles for creating emotional involvement in a subject, stimulating interest, or raising issues such as social impact.

Some science centers present theater on a regular basis, alternating plays based on demand and actor availability. Others use the technique to complement a particular temporary exhibition. The plays typically are performed either in an auditorium, in a less formal open space, or within an exhibit related to the topic. Expenses are driven primarily by the cost of actors, paid either by salary or on a contractual basis per performance. To reduce costs or to experiment with theater, science centers may wish to pursue collaborations with existing theater companies or with drama programs at local universities and schools.

The plays in this anthology were solicited through a request made to ASTC member institutions. The plays submitted for consideration were reviewed by a panel that included Tessa Bridal, Science Museum of Minnesota; Kathryn James, Applied Theatre Techniques, Culver City, California; and Susan McCormick, ASTC Publications Coordinator. The criteria for selection were overall quality of script, potential audience impact, and value to science-technology centers. Making the selections was not an easy task, and I would like to thank the reviewers for their efforts.

We hope that this publication not only will encourage the use of theater by other science centers, but also will stimulate the writing and production of many more works that will lead to volume two of *Science on Stage!*

David A. Ucko
President, Kansas City Museum
Co-Chair, ASTC Publications Committee

FOREWORD

I was frankly delighted when Dave Ucko of the ASTC Publications Committee invited me to edit this volume. It seemed timely to publish a volume of science plays to celebrate the twentieth anniversary of the use of theater in museums, and to acknowledge the accomplishments of those who have worked hard to promote its use.

Foremost among these must be Sondra Quinn, now executive director of the Orlando Science Center, who 20 years ago introduced a one-person puppet show on the Anthropology Floor at the Science Museum of Minnesota, and dedicated the next 15 years of her life to establishing the use of theater in museums as a successful and respected educational tool.

The plays we chose to include here represent several styles—monologues, broad comedy, vignettes—and their content is not necessarily linked to an exhibit. They could be used to enhance exhibits on the subjects covered in the play, or be presented independently.

When assessing the merits of plays, the criteria I apply is largely subjective. Do the characters come to life? Do they keep me engaged and interested? Have my insights been broadened by the piece? There are, however, certain objective standards I believe a museum theater piece should meet: Does the piece achieve its own stated goals? Is the information accurate and clear? Is the writer master of his or her chosen style?

Two questions we need to ask ourselves when we're considering the use of theater in our institutions are: what do we mean by "theater"? and why do we want to do it?

There is a vast difference between theater and theatrical techniques. Theatrical techniques can include costumed interpreters, lighting and sound effects, props, and sets. The use of these various techniques, however, does not constitute theater. Museum theater has been defined as an activity that:
- relates to an institution's exhibits, mission, or associated issues;
- is performed by actors assuming a character other than their own; and
- is performed by theater professionals.

Within this framework there are many styles of performance to be explored, from a straightforward rendering of a historical character to a puppet show; or the use of dance, music, clowning, or mime. Pieces can be interactive and involve the audience, or maintain the

7

"fourth wall" illusion characteristic of traditional theater settings. They can be performed in auditoriums or in the exhibit halls themselves.

Your reasons for doing theater will determine most of your choices: whether or not you charge admission to your performances; where and when you will perform; who will administer the production(s); how hiring will be done; how and if you will evaluate the results; and who your audience will be. When making these decisions, it is wise to consult with others who have traveled the same route and, whenever possible, visit institutions using theater to inform yourself thoroughly on your choices.

At the Science Museum of Minnesota, theater is used to aid the public in seeing that science is relevant to them; to demystify science and break through prejudice directed toward scientific study; to provide an atmosphere in which visitors can easily pursue informal learning; to provide up-to-date, accurate scientific information; to present science as a social process; and to make our museum come alive.

It has become evident to us that performances draw and hold crowds, and that audiences find their interests peaked by the subjects seen in performance and ask more questions about that subject than those who have not attended a performance. They then spend more time visiting related exhibits.

Over the years, the program has grown to include several actors and playwrights, supported, initially, by grants obtained for that purpose. Seven years ago, acknowledging that the use of theater had become an integral part of SMM's educational mission, the Museum created a theater department with a budget that was part of the Museum's general operating fund. In response to an increasing interest in the use of theater, the Museum also hosts an annual workshop on the use of theater as an interpretive technique.

As you will see as you read the plays in this volume, the uses to which theater can be put are limited only by our imaginations.

It is my belief that museum theater can embody the best in education and entertainment. If we agree with Samuel Taylor Coleridge that "the proper and immediate object of science is the acquirement, or communication of truth;" and "the proper and immediate object of poetry [or theater] is the communication of immediate pleasure," then science theater is a perfect blend for achieving both those ends.

Tessa Bridal
Director, Theatre Department
Science Museum of Minnesota

CENTER STAGE IN THE MUSEUM: USING THEATER TO PRESENT THE ISSUES

by Tessa Bridal

At the Science Museum of Minnesota, and in museums worldwide, we are in the privileged position of being able to reach millions of people with our work. It is a privilege we must not take lightly. As our world becomes increasingly complex, and as educators are forced to grapple with a range of often conflicting information about our environment, our society, our future, and the global implications of our scientific and technological advances, museums should be leaders in providing forums for public discussion. If indeed we preserve objects because the past can teach us valuable lessons about the future, then we must release the information in a way that both challenges our conclusions and encourages flights of thoughtful fancy.

When I am asked to describe my work as director of the museum's Theatre Department, I usually reply, "I use theater to interpret the museum's exhibits." I explain further that behind every object on display are the people who made it, used it, or were affected by it. Through theater, we can bring those people to life, and by doing so we can spark greater interest in the object itself. Eighteen years ago, educator Sondra Quinn, who is now executive director of the Orlando Science Center, concluded that some lively methods of interpretation would certainly enhance the museums' exhibits. She proposed using theater to interpret both the exhibits and the purposes behind them, and she started experimenting with ways of enlivening and humanizing the artifacts on display. The resulting theater program was extremely popular. Funded at first by special grants, the program was made part of the museum's general operating budget and a department was created for it.

When I joined the program as director in 1984, I became involved in developing more than 40 original theater presentations, which ranged from historical monologues depicting scientists such as Marie Curie to pieces involving several actors performing folk dances and games from around the world. The experience was fascinating and rewarding for the program staff, because we had the opportunity to explore such a diverse spectrum of subjects.

Soon I began to wonder whether we could also use our theater pieces to examine the largely unexplored and thorny issues that technology, history, and human development raise. Should it be a museum's mission to warn of dangers, to encourage thoughtful progress, to raise doubts—and perhaps even fears—about our future? In my mind, the answer to that question was a resounding yes. Not as clear to me was how we would approach our curators with this notion. Ideas for theater pieces come both from the curators of our exhibits and from the playwrights, directors, and actors who interpret the exhibits. After the appropriate curator and I discuss and approve a proposal, it is assigned to a playwright for development, with the curator acting as the content specialist. Stereotypes of curators and artists play an important role in determining the curator-playwright relationship. Curators are often portrayed as rather stuffy and narrow-minded individuals, more interested in their collections than in the collections' effect on the public they are supposedly serving. Artists, in contrast, are seen as irresponsible, temperamental types who view accuracy as a curb to their creativity and who turn exhibit halls into circuses. Like most stereotypes, these do not hold up under close scrutiny.

ACT I: MEDICAL TECHNOLOGY

Having subscribed to the curator stereotype, I was somewhat surprised to encounter excitement, interest, and support when I approach our curators with my proposal to present Kurt Vonnegut's unproduced one-act play, "Fortitude." The play addresses, in somewhat farcical Vonnegut style, the issues surrounding the effects of medical technology on the prolongation of life. Two of the physicians in the play are self-serving and, to put it mildly, eccentric. The third physician questions his colleagues' actions but takes no stand against them. The play is not a scientifically balanced presentation of the issues, but I argued that scientific balance was not necessarily what audiences would expect of Vonnegut and that we should not refuse his generous offer to support our program by allowing us to use his play without royalty charges.

After the project was approved, we turned to our next concern: audience reaction. What would our visitors say when confronted with a mad doctor and a disembodied talking head kept alive by medical technology? To find out, we organized an informal survey of our audience. In a one-page questionnaire, we asked what educational and entertainment value "Fortitude" had and whether people's curiosity about the issues had been aroused. We also solicited general comments on the play. "Fortitude" was judged as having a high degree of both educational and entertainment value, and it had indeed aroused people's curiosity. Not one of the 500 respondents objected to the presentation of the issues, and they overwhelmingly supported the museum for examining them.

We learned more about our audience's reactions by holding a special performance of the play, followed by a discussion with medical ethicists, attorneys, and religious representatives who were asked to address the issues from their particular perspectives. The audience of more than 100 people participated actively in the discussion and were persuaded to leave only when we had to close the museum's doors for the night.

ACT II: WOMEN IN SCIENCE

With the success of "Fortitude" under our belts, we began to plan programs for an exhibit on women in science. We formed an all-female committee, consisting of local scientists, educators, business executives, and others interested in the topic, to advise the museum on programs and events to accompany the exhibit. The committee met regularly for several weeks and strongly recommended that the museum develop a play addressing issues of education and career opportunities for women.

We found evidence of the need for such a program in a report from the Minnesota Alliance for Science, which explained, "Up to sixth grade, girls in Minnesota perform just as well as boys in math and science tests. But in junior high, girls' scores start to drop." This difference in scores is attributed to "signals from family and peers that girls don't have to be good at math and science." The findings of a Minnesota Youth Poll further supported the need for a play on women's issues:

- Almost all respondents thought that the different treatment afforded to males and females at home and school had a negative impact on girls and a positive one on boys.
- Two-thirds of both males and females accepted the Cinderella myth, that most young women want to marry handsome men who will take care of them for the rest of their lives so they won't have to work.
- Seventy percent of males and 60 percent of females approved and endorsed the Supermom model, successful in career, child rearing, homemaking, community affairs, and in keeping her husband happy.

11

Given such findings, it is not surprising that only 12 percent of today's scientists are women.

How could we address all of these issues in one 30-minute play? We assigned the project to playwright Heidi Arneson, who proceeded to invite a large group of women to her home. She asked them to talk about their experiences at school and at work, their choices and what prompted them, their fears, their failures, and their successes. The play Arneson wrote was based on these women's real-life experiences. "Sara the Scientist" is a series of vignettes tracing a woman's life from birth through marriage, motherhood, and the attainment of a scientific career. It starts as Sara's father takes her to a toy store to buy blocks and finds himself having to persuade the store clerk that blocks are appropriate for a baby girl. Another scene involves a junior high school math contest for which the first prize is a tie clasp. The play ends with Sara's decision to leave a dead-end position as a research assistant to find a job that has "responsibility and room to grow."

We surveyed the audiences for "Sara the Scientist," but on a smaller scale than our "Fortitude" survey. Sixty-eight people—about 20 percent of those who saw the play—completed the survey form, which consisted of five questions. The female respondents included 32 women over age 19, 12 teenagers ages 13 to 19, and nine girls ages eight to 12. Twelve men responded, 10 men over 19 and 2 in their late teens.

Our first question was, Did any of Sara's experiences relate to you personally? As might be expected, younger girls did not relate to Sara's experiences as readily as grown women did. Still, almost 50 percent (4) of the girls 12 years old and under answered yes. Among teenage girls, this percentage increased to 66 percent, or 8 of the 12 women. Eighty-five percent (17) of the women in the 20-to-40 age range and 100 percent of the 12 women over age 40 said they could relate to Sara's experiences. Only 3 men in the survey, or 25 percent, said they could personally relate to Sara's experiences.

Question 2 in our survey was, Did watching this piece enhance your enjoyment of the exhibit on women in science? With the exception of one 10-year-old girl, all the respondents answered yes.

In question 3, we asked whether the audience members' perceptions about women were affected by the theater presentation of the exhibit. Not all the survey respondents answered this question, but of those who did, 55 percent (26 out of 47) agreed that either the play, the exhibit, or both had affected their perceptions. Most of the women and girls felt that their perceptions had been affected by the theater piece and the exhibit; however, 9 said the play was especially affecting. Only one woman (age 33) singled out the exhibit in this way, and she indicated that she was already familiar with the information in the theater piece.

It is interesting to note that of the 10 men responding to this question, eight said their perceptions had been affected. Six indicated that both the play and the exhibit had been responsible. Three singled out the theater piece, and two (both over age 50) singled out the exhibit. (These numbers do not quite add up because of discrepancies in survey answers.)

In response to question 5—Do you think the museum should continue to develop theater pieces?—the participants unanimously said yes.

We can draw several subjective conclusions from this informal survey.

- "Sara the Scientist" was an important component of the *Women in Science and Engineering* exhibition.
- On the whole, women related more easily to the play than did men, but the exhibit and the play together successfully presented new information about women in science to both sexes, particularly to males.
- The play was a valuable tool in presenting this new information.
- The enthusiastic response to question 5 indicates that presentations similar to "Sara" could be valuable educational tools and museum attractions in the future.

ACT III: NUCLEAR WINTER

Having proved to our satisfaction that audiences responded enthusiastically to the presentation of issues through a combination of an exhibit and a theatrical piece, we then faced the challenge of addressing an issue for which there was no exhibit: nuclear winter. Theater seemed a useful tool with which to examine the nuclear winter theory and discuss some of the peripheral issues of preparedness for nuclear war and its consequences.

Through a longer-than-usual rehearsal period, the acting company, with playwright Marilyn Seven, improvised on ideas for a play that would address the content and the context of nuclear winter. Working with this subject was no easy task. We swung between scenarios of despairing drama and far-fetched farce. Finally, we came up with a format that allowed for some of both.

The setting for "Coming of Nuclear Age" is a town meeting to which two speakers are invited—a peace activist and a representative from the Federal Emergency Management Agency. Members of the audience are also involved as participants. The peace activist asserts that it is a waste of resources to plan for an unsurvivable disaster and that the government should instead use those resources to ensure that peace is maintained and nuclear weapons are abolished. The government representative claims that it would be irresponsible to neglect survival plans when no one knows for certain that there will be no survivors and that the government must be prepared for every eventuality.

No survey was conducted for this presentation, but the audience participated actively during the play, asking questions of both speakers and occasionally siding strongly with one or the other. Audience members were often overwhelmed by both the newness and the significance of the information, and they needed time to assimilate what they had heard. Our usual technique of inviting questions and visiting with audiences after a performance is not always successful with pieces that address such emotional issues. (This was sometimes true with "Fortitude" as well.)

In my mind, there is no question about the responsibility museums bear toward the objects they exhibit. That responsibility goes beyond the preservation and study of the objects to their significance in the lives of all who are affected by them. Whether the object is an ancient hoe, a painting, or a piece of technological innovation, its creation affected our world, and we all share in it.

I am proud to be involved in interpreting the knowledge and research we display in our exhibit halls. Most of my work involves exalting that knowledge and research, but I relish opportunities to scrutinize the consequences. There is no basis for the fear that by raising the issues we will appear to be taking sides. (Perhaps, on some issues, we should.) There is every indication, however, that the public appreciates a responsible approach, one that presents the facts and raises questions about where those facts lead us.

Reprinted with permission from *The Journal of Museum Education*, "Museums as a Social Instrument Revisited," Winter 1989.

ALICE IN
NUMBERLAND

 **Robin L. Scott**

© Robin L. Scott, 1987

Above: A step-on trash can was fashioned into a teapot by soft-sculpting a cover of tea-cozy quilting and silver lamé.

Right: A thorough scavenging of remainder tables at fabric outlets led to the creation of this soft-sculpted Inchworm puppet.

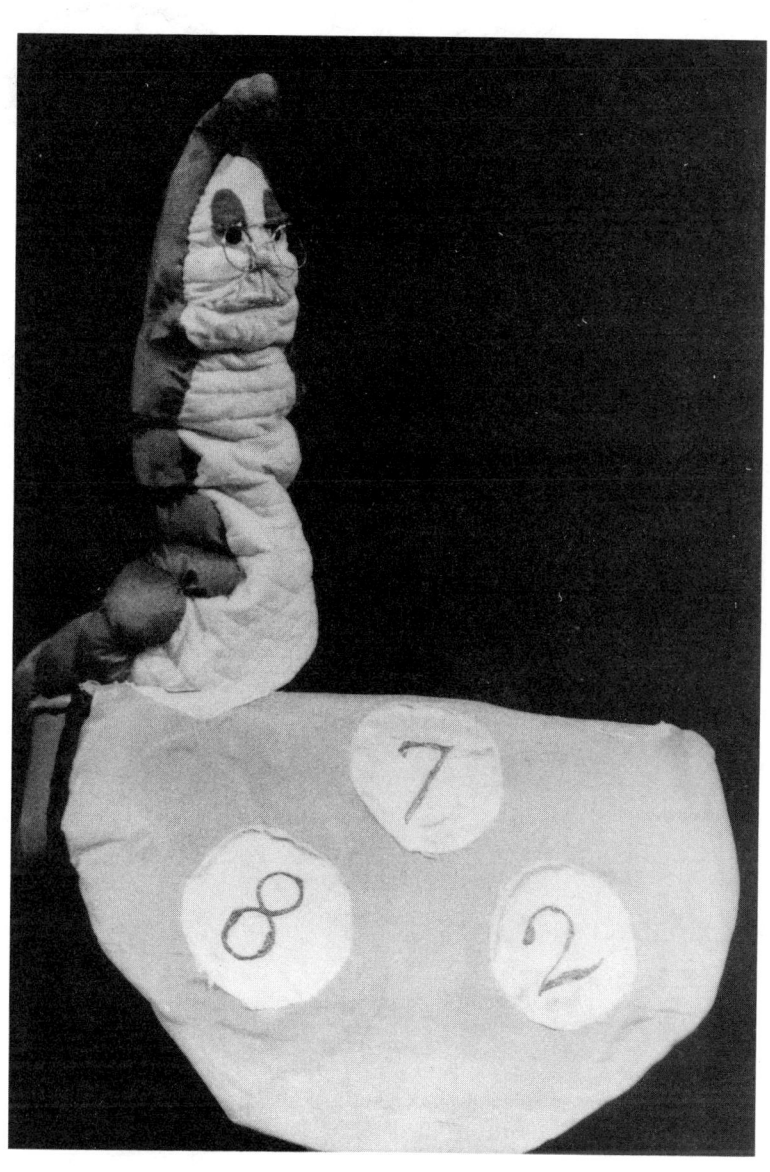

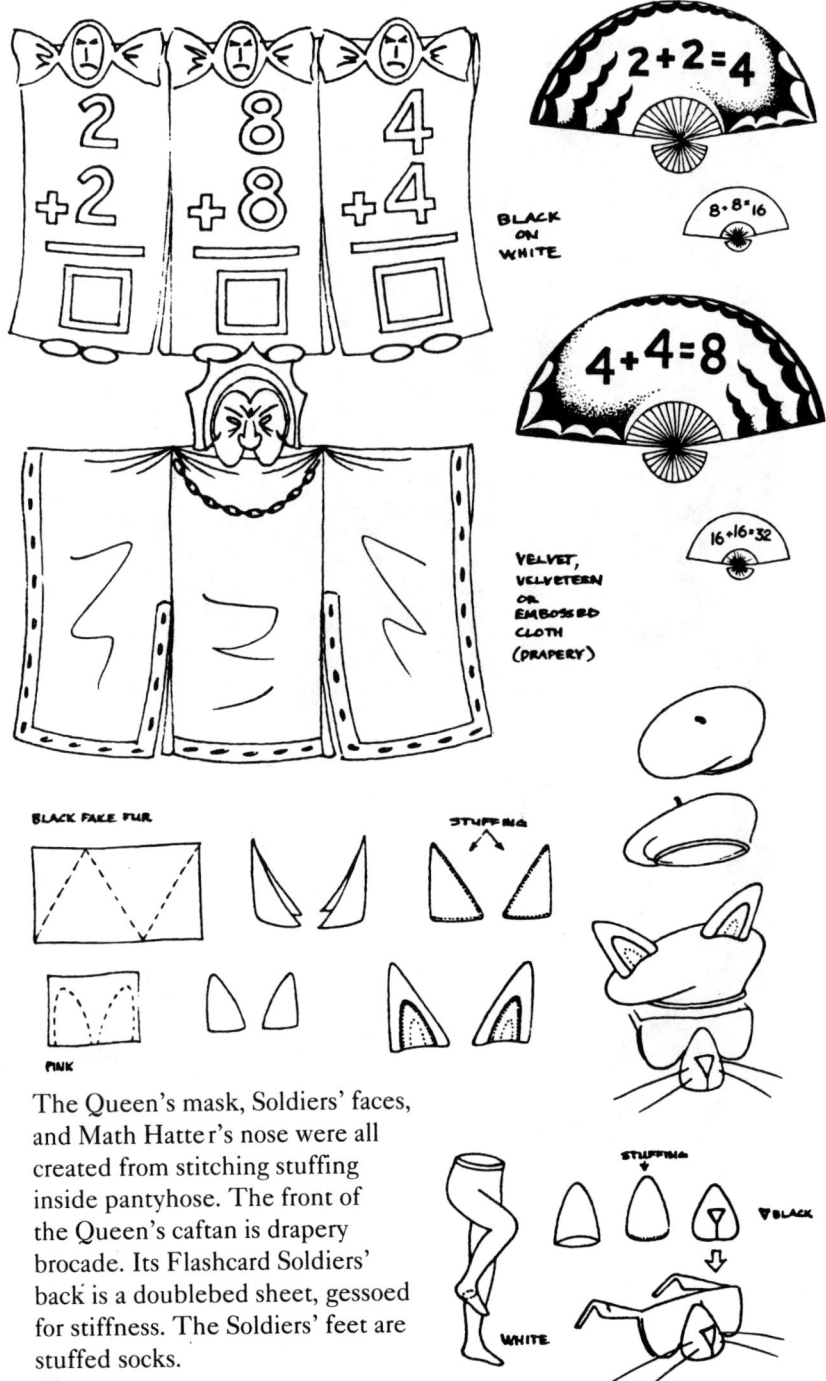

The Queen's mask, Soldiers' faces, and Math Hatter's nose were all created from stitching stuffing inside pantyhose. The front of the Queen's caftan is drapery brocade. Its Flashcard Soldiers' back is a doublebed sheet, gessoed for stiffness. The Soldiers' feet are stuffed socks.

PLAYWRIGHT'S NOTES

This play came into being almost by accident. There was no commission to create such a piece, as there had been for the two scripts with which the theater program began its shows at the California Museum of Science and Industry (CMSI). In fact, I'd not been hired as a writer but as an actress. But the embryonic program needed plays for as many exhibits as possible. Since *Mathematica* is the oldest continuing permanent exhibition at CMSI, it seemed a natural subject. It is from material in the exhibition that most of the play's mathematical references are drawn.

Also, some outside inspiration existed—a young lady of my acquaintance, long a math whiz, suddenly at the outset of her ninth-grade year reported bleakly that she could no longer do algebra, etc. Her father suggested she ask her teacher for help, an idea which appeared to be a revelation to her. When she followed the suggestion (her teacher was so thrilled, he practically wept) her subsequent success not only overcame her math anxiety, but also led her to become a sort of ombudsman for her fellow students. It seems that, in most cases, the last thing a student wants to do is ask a teacher for help, fearing to appear stupid. Once students start communicating in this way, all sorts of magical possibilities open up.

Another source of inspiration was my long, affectionate familiarity with a book called *The Annotated Alice*. It was here I'd learned that Charles Dodgson was a dean of mathematics and that many hidden mathematical/logical concepts exist in his two Alice stories. It seemed a made-to-order framework.

With no deadline, then, and constantly distracted by the needs of the ongoing program (not just performance but prop, costume, set, and sound) I began recording into my cassette player first thoughts, then scene concepts, then whole scenes and passages. The first completed bit was "Algebrarocky" which was turned into a short monologue for a special day-long tour. This monologue was then performed for some months as the complete play continued to evolve. At least one of the scenes, a logic sequence with a character called Elegant Proof and modeled after the White Knight, was never completed and remains in the recesses of the author's imagination, to be added if the play ever needs to be lengthened.

At a certain point, the script was done and was submitted to the Manager of Education. It was circulated among the curators and officers of the museum who passed it for content. A small amount of money existed in the department's restricted account for set, costume, and props. Now what was needed was a deadline. This occurred in the form of the Los Angeles Fringe Festival, September 1987. The Education Manager listed the piece for presentation and the heat was on.

PRODUCTION HISTORY AND NOTES

"Alice in Numberland" has been presented almost continuously since its premiere at the September 1987 Los Angeles Fringe Festival. It was then that the show received the company's only review to date, an excellent notice in the *Los Angeles Times*.

During the Christmas and Easter breaks, Alice is performed daily, otherwise playing two to four performances per week during the school touring season. It has been hired to perform for the last three Literacy Fairs, bringing some $1,500 in fees into the program account. "Alice in Numberland" has been cleared by audition to be presented in the Los Angeles Unified School District should a touring program be implemented. It has proved to be popular with a wide range of grades as well as weekend (family) audiences.

The show was videotaped by a local public access cable station where it aired for a number of months and still runs occasionally. The station also submitted the program for an ACE award in the children's category. The museum foundation has included copies of the tape in a number of grant request packages.

With minor repairs and upgrades, the various production elements have continued in use for the two-and-a-half years since the play's premiere. Some design elements have proved to be not only durable but amazingly flexible. The Actor's black pajama costume, for example, has been worn by five actors who differed considerably in height and build.

The original set construction and design, suggested from a doodle by the author, was created by a company actor and student/stage manager. Scrap wood from exhibits and a 50-cent-a-yard sale on unbleached muslin kept its materials costs low. Similar finds from the remainder tables of various fabric outlets led to the design of the Inchworm puppet: tummy and face of quilted pale green, back and topknot of stretchy bright green, stuffed and sculpted into characteristic caterpillar shapes. Soft-sculpture techniques, gained by observation of work in a local gallery, were used to create the puppet's haughty expression.

After a used step-on trash can was finally tracked down at a medical supplies outlet, the tech crew (of one) pointed out that we lacked the tools necessary for him to weld a spout and handle onto anything metal; he suggested that the author soft-sculpt a teapot slipcover of tea-cozy quilting and silver lame, left over from a prior show. It was at this point that the overall soft-sculpture look of this production was decided upon.

The Queen's mask, Soldiers' faces and Math Hatter's nose were all created from stitching stuffing inside panty hose. The crown of the Math Hatter's Hat is purple quilted material over a bucket; the brim form was cut from a plastic cowboy hat.

Not everything had to be created, however. The Dormouse, who had originally been one member of a hugging pair, was purchased for 35 cents at a secondhand shop for infants. The March Hare, perfect for the part but an expensive toy, suddenly showed up at a sidewalk sale at a third of his normal retail price due to mistreatment. We cleaned him up, sewed a teacup and a foam-rubber doughnut to his paws, stuffed him into the hat and were all set.

The front of the Queen's caftan is drapery brocade, a fortuitous donation; the ermine trim is fashioned from white, ribbed fake fur and locks from a black wig. Its Flashcard Soldiers' back is a double-bed sheet, gessoed for stiffness. The Soldiers' feet are stuffed socks, their cowls a happy find of black velvet sale yardage.

Alice's original dress was found at a thrift store, as was her pinafore, fashioned from a muslin sun dress. Only the Actor's black costume was sewn from a pattern, a modified Pierrot, until the present Alice dress was added, made from a modified Minnie Mouse costume pattern. It was finished just in time to be seen by the Duke and Duchess of York as Alice entertained waiting crowds of children prior to the royal visit to the museum.

PRODUCTION RIGHTS

This script is available to nonprofit institutions for production.

In-house lease, unlimited performances	$500/year
In-house lease, limited run performances	$100 script + 3 performances $ 25/additional performance
Off-site (paid tour, no in-house)	$100 script fee + $ 25/performance

NOTE: If an institution leases the script on a yearly basis, limited or unlimited, and subsequently tours that production, only the $25/show royalty would be charged on the touring performances. No additional script fee would apply as long as the annual lease held.

Detailed production information is separately available. For rights and further information, contact Robin L. Scott, 615 Santa Clara Avenue, Venice, CA 90291; 213/392-2370.

ALICE IN NUMBERLAND

SET: A backdrop consisting of a four-paneled screen with two floor braces. The two side panels are hinged and double-sided so that they can be closed to first show a classroom wall with blackboard, and later opened to become a larger blackboard with Numberland scenery drawn in colored chalk. One panel has a practical hole for C.C. Cat's head.

The second piece is a practical school desk with a drop panel which transforms it into a giant mushroom. Both pieces should be simply, even childishly, painted.

"Alice" is a two-actor, eight-character *(eleven, if one counts the SOL-DIERS who do not speak)* play.

ALICE: Classic Tenniel-cum-Disney costume; long hair, held by bandeau, blue dress with cap or puff sleeves, pinafore, white stockings, Mary Janes.

ACTOR: Plays all the other characters; wears simple, black pajamas to blend with background and contrast with character accoutrements.

INCHWORM: Arm-long green puppet, big eyes with spectacles, lots of little legs. Dry and academic.

CHESHIRE COOL CAT: Beatnik beret with cat ears, detachable tail, sunglasses with vinyl cat-nose attached.

MATH HATTER: Huge top hat with 25c tag, large glasses with big soft-sculpture nose, collar with big bow tie.

MARCH HARE: Bunny puppet hidden in Hatter's top hat which Hatter pulls out and wears on hand. Puppet has teacup on one hand, doughnut on the other.

DORMOUSE: Stuffed or painted mouse, located in step-on trash can which has spout and handle to look like a large teapot. Pops up when pedal is pressed.

QUEEN: Wears brightly colored caftan and crown. On the back of the caftan are painted three FLASH-CARD SOLDIERS, one on each extended arm, one down the back.

MR. DODGSON: Old-fashioned don's collar, spectacles.

(Scene opens with Alice's desk in front of screen to classroom position. MR. DODGSON enters, trailed by ALICE carrying oversized book bag.)

MR. DODGSON: Alice, I am afraid you may not go home until you have finished your arithmetic problems. If you need me, I shall be in my office grading papers. *(Exits behind the screen)*

ALICE: Well, this is not fair. Mr. Dodgson, you are a cruel, heartless tutor, keeping me after school. Oh, all right, I know I didn't do my math assignment. I couldn't, that's all. Math's not for me! I don't know how to do these problems. Anyway, why should I do math? I won't ever need it. And if I do, I'll use a calculator. If Mr. Dodgson would only let me use one. Although, I don't really know how to use one yet. Oh, I'm so confused. And so-o-o sleepy. And this math book has no pictures. *(Puts her head down on desk.)* Two plus two, where are you? You—answer...come back...come back... *(Already asleep, reaches out as if to catch an escaping answer and slides from the desk to the floor beneath)*

ACTOR, dressed in black, changes classroom to NUMBERLAND screen, desk to giant mushroom. Sits, and has INCHWORM puppet peek over mushroom top at Alice beneath.

INCHWORM: Hello-o-o.

ALICE: What? Who...?

INCHWORM: What sort of Mathematician are you?

ALICE: I'm not a mathematician at all. I'm just a little girl.

INCHWORM: That doesn't add up. A girl can be a mathematician, too.

ALICE: Are you a mathematician? Who are you? And where am I?

INCHWORM: One thing at a time. If you try to jump too far ahead, you'll only fall behind. First question?

ALICE: *(Confused)* I suppose, Where am I? is most important.

INCHWORM: Good question! When you know where you are, you can find out where you're going. Numberland. Next question.

ALICE: But...

INCHWORM: Next question. Only so much time to learn. Then you're on your own.

ALICE: Who are you?

INCHWORM: Inchworm. Arithmetic doer, measuring marigolds a specialty. *(Gives her his card.)*

ALICE: And you're a mathematician?

INCHWORM: We're all mathematicians here in Numberland.

ALICE: Not I. I'm just confused and...

INCHWORM: Then start with what you know. Two and two? *(Inches large fan out of desk to ALICE who opens it to reveal 2 + 2 = 4 painted on one side.)*

ALICE: Are four, but...

INCHWORM: Four and four? *(Second fan emerges with 4 + 4 = 8.)*

ALICE: Are eight, only...

INCHWORM: Eight and eight? *(First fan turns to show 8 + 8 = 16.)*

ALICE: Are sixteen... *(Turns fan to 16 + 16 = 32.)*

INCHWORM: And sixteen and sixteen are thirty-two. Again.

(ALICE and INCHWORM sing through chorus together. Fans turn appropriately to encourage audience to sing with INCHWORM as ALICE sings counterpoint verse over them.)

ALICE: Inchworm, Inchworm, measuring the marigolds, You and your arithmetic will probably go far. Inchworm, Inchworm, measuring the marigolds, You would think you'd stop and see how beautiful they are.

(ALICE takes chorus with audience as INCHWORM sings second counterpoint verse)

INCHWORM: There's a beauty you can't see, hidden in your memory. Everything you learn today will help you find your way. Learn simple things first, soon you'll know just how far your mind can grow. Now's the time to open doors for futures to be yours. *(Fans are transferred to ACTOR'S hand, become butterfly wings which allow former Inchworm to fly away, disappearing behind screen).*

ALICE: *(Continues to sing one last chorus, unaware of defection of Inchworm.)* So, knowing my math tables will help me find my way? My way where? Out of Numberland? Inchworm? Inchworm? *(Hunts all about mushroom.)* Oh... *(Plumps down, crying inconsolably. ACTOR puts head through hole in screen as CHESHIRE COOL CAT.)*

C.C. CAT: Be cool, little mama. Be cool.

ALICE: Oh! *(Scrambles to her feet, wiping away tears. CAT enters and taps her on the shoulder)* You startled me.

C.C. CAT: Well, the Cheshire Cool Cat moves softly. Little cat feet, you dig?

ALICE: But you just appeared out of nowhere.

C.C. CAT: Everybody gotta be somewhere. But you look a little outa place. You lost or something?

ALICE: Oh, yes. Everything around here is math, you see, and I can barely do my own arithmetic problems at school. And I know it's going to get even harder. *(Building up steam for another crying jag)* I've heard about algebra!

C.C. CAT: *(Pulls out multiple Magician's handkerchief to forestall her tears)* Whoa! You get too far ahead of yourself. First learn your ABC's; then you can *deal* with the "X."

ALICE: What do you mean?

C.C. CAT: *(Shows various arithmetic functions on hankies)* Why, you start adding and subtracting, which'll lead up to multiplying, when the time comes, after which you can divide! When all that makes sense, it's easy to find ol' Mr. X.

ALICE: *(Confused by his patter)* But what if it doesn't make sense?

C.C. CAT: Then ask for help. That's what teachers are for. Here, I'll show you. *(Opens book bag and begins handing Alice rhythm instruments)* Take some of these and get these cats to sit in. (To audience) You'll all give us a hand, won't you?

(As ALICE continues to pass out instruments, CAT pulls out three slates which read "Equation 1/5 = 4/X; cross-multiply 2X = (4x5); Divide by 2 2X/2 = 20/2." He does not reveal the printed sides to the audience)

C.C. CAT: I need three very special volunteers to come here and help ol' Cheshire Cool Cat. *(Chooses three volunteers, giving each a slate and coaching them to keep it turned from the audience until he gives each a signal. During this, ALICE covers by explaining that those who don't have rhythm instruments might help out by clapping hands to the upcoming beat.)* And here it is *(Pulls stuffed wrestling dummy labeled "The Masked X" out of bag)* the Masked X, bane of math students for generations. Now, little mama, it's time for you to wrestle with your first Algebra problem. *(Tosses dummy to ALICE who struggles with it during the following)* And here's the beat. *("Rap" beat is heard)* And here we go:

There was a man in Arabia
Who earned the world of Math's respects
When he came up with the concept "Algebra"
And figured how to find the elusive "X."

The dreaded, sneaky slimy "X"
Did hide in the Algebra equation
(First slate is revealed)
To frighten students with special effects,
Not a body snatcher, just a mind invasion.

(To Alice, whom he helps from a tangled "hold")
Beware the dread "X," little one,
Don't let it get the best of you!
Beware confusion that can come
When you don't know just what to do!

You'll take the math that you will learn,
How to multiply *(Show second slate)*
and to divide, *(Show third slate)*
And each equation you will turn
Inside out till X is alone on one side!

(ALICE flips dummy's cape to reveal "X=10", then pounces on him and "pins" him as C.C. CAT counts as a referee.)

One, Two; one, two, *Three*! You are through!
That variable "X" is now so easy to see.
You've got it done, and when you test the sum
You'll know you're right invariably.
(Holds Alice's hand up in "champ" pose.)

And have you solved Algebrarock?
Well, take a bow, you sharp, smart kids.
(Returns volunteers to seats on applause.)
You knew you should, we knew you could.
Now aren't you glad you did?

You're brilliant and that slimy "X"
Will cower and tremble on the page.
All flimsy its attempts to hex
Students so savvy and so sage.

(C.C. CAT and ALICE flip dummy over the set out of sight.)

ALICE: That was fun! I don't feel half so scared and unhappy now.

C.C.CAT: Math anxiety, that's all. Like a big scary monster till you look it in the eye and ask for help. *(Pulls out magic bag with Mad Ball which he brandishes.)*

ALICE: Oh!

C.C. CAT: And you always feel good when you s-t-r-e-t-c-h out your mind a little and wrestle a problem till it's solved. *(Makes ball disappear into bag.)* If all problems were math problems, this would be an easy life.

ALICE: That's right. I still have a big problem. I'm still lost. Which way do you think I should go?

C.C. CAT: Well, *that* way leads to the Math Hatter s place, *(Points across his body)* and *that* way leads to the March Hare's *(Crosses arm by pointing in opposite direction).* Choose whichever you like. *(Spins to untangle arms, ending front, hands clasped)* They live together.

ALICE: You mean both ways go to the same place?

C.C. CAT: Yeah! They're commutative. Kinda like 3 + 2 is the same as 2 + 3.

ALICE: So when I go these ways *(With CAT)* I'm a commuter!

C.C. CAT: You're a commuter! But it only works for addition, multiplication, and going to a Math Tea Party.

ALICE: A Tea Party! Oh, I love tea parties! Are you going too?

C.C. CAT: No, I have to be disappearing now. *(Tosses Alice his bag)* Collect those instruments for me, would you please? Oh, and don't forget what you've learned. I'll catch you later for my bag—at the Queen's.

ALICE: *(Preoccupied with the bag, does not see him exit)* The Queen's? What do you mean? Where's he gone? *(Looks around, into bag, etc.)*

Cheshire Cat? Cheshire Cool Cat? C.C.? Oh, it is so aggravating when creatures keep appearing and disappearing without so much as a by-your-leave. *(Walks through audience collecting instruments)* Thank you, just in there, please *(Ad lib thanks)*. Remember what I've learned, that's all he cares about.

Well, what have I learnt? That everybody is a mathematician? Well, I suppose that's true. A cook needs to do proportions; a shopkeeper has to know percentages; mothers and fathers have to keep the budget. So, even if I don't decide to be an astrophysicist, math might come in handy. And I've learnt that simple math's a stepping stone to higher math. If I just keep up by asking questions, I'll know what to do when I get there. *(As Alice has worked her way through audience, ACTOR has appeared as MATH HATTER with trash-can teapot containing DORMOUSE and MARCH HARE puppet concealed in hat.)* Oh look! I've got here! What a big pot!

MATH HATTER: No room, no room!

ALICE: Why, of course there's room. There's only you, and look what a big tea pot you've got!

MATH HATTER: Just enough for three.

ALICE: But it's only we two.

MATH HATTER: It's only we three! You don't count.

ALICE: How rude! I do count.

M. HATTER: Then count this! *(Dances soft shoe, trying to kick Alice out at every opportunity.)* Three for Two and Two for Three. Who asked you to come for Tea? It's just we three, which leaves you one alone!

ALICE: But you're just one. Where are the other two?

M HATTER: Me, the March Hare and the Dormouse.

ALICE: I don't see any hare or any mouse.

M. HATTER: Oh, that's right, Hare is under my hat.

29

ALICE: Well, of course your hair is under your hat...

M. HATTER: No, no, no. I guess I'll just have to pull hare out! *(Removes hat and pulls out March Hare, a bunny puppet which has a tea cup and doughnut.)*

ALICE: Oh, I see. That sort of hare. And the dormouse?

M. HATTER: In the teapot, of course. *(Pushes on can pedal, top pops open revealing Dormouse, then snaps shut.)*

ALICE: EEK! Well, I suppose I really don't want any tea after all, thank you very much, I'll just be on my way...

M. HATTER: Do you know any fractions?

ALICE: *(Stops, startled)* Well, I haven't got to fractions yet in school...

M. HATTER: So you can't sing.

ALICE: Yes, of course, I love to sing.

M. HATTER: Then you do know fractions. No more excuses.

ALICE: But...

M. HATTER: There are four of us, correct? *(Dormouse pops up.)*

ALICE: I suppose...

M. HATTER: So if "us" is one whole, each is one quarter, right?

ALICE: You mean...

M. HATTER: Four quarter time!

As HARE: Four quarter time?

As DORMOUSE: *(Each time Dormouse is to speak, lid pops open)* Four quarter time!

ALICE: Four quarter time?

M. HATTER: How old are you? Seven?

ALICE: Going on eight.

M. HATTER: Good. You be eighths. Dormouse'll be "halves" because he's not all there, Hare'll be whole 'cause there's one in his doughnut; and I'll be quarter 'cause it's on my hat. Begin.

HARE: *(Sings, holding note for four counts)* Who-o-o-ole.

DORMOUSE: *(Pops up on each two count.)* Half! Half!

M. HATTER: Quarter, quarter, quarter, quarter.

ALICE: Eighth, eighth, eighth, eighth, eighth, eighth, eighth, eighth.

M. HATTER: *(To first section of audience)* Everybody here to here, you're with Hare. Sing "whole" for four counts. Ready?

HARE: Who-o-o-ole. (With audience.)

ALICE: I see! Everybody from here to here, sing "half" when the Dormouse pops up. Here we go! *(Works the Dormouse for the song.)*

DORMOUSE: Half! Half!

M. HATTER: Now this quarter, you're with me. Sing "quarter" on each beat. *(Counts four beats with his "non-Hare" hands as he sings)* Quarter, quarter, quarter, quarter.

ALICE: Oh! My section had better be the best of all—we've got the hard part. Do you think you can do it? Quick time on eighths; ready go! Eighth, eighth, eighth, eighth, eighth, eighth, eighth, eighth.

M. HATTER: Start again, ready go! Whole, half, half, quarter, quarter, quarter, quarter, eighth, eighth, eighth, eighth, eighth, eighth, eighth, eighth.

(They encourage the audience to sing the chant/song as the different characters. Alice continues to lead the full chorus as Hatter begins to march off chanting the following)

>We're off to see the Queen,
>Although she's awfully mean;
>It's there we must be seen,
>So we're off to see the Queen,
>We're off to see the Queen...

(HATTER marches off to disappear behind screen. ALICE, still leading her section in "eighths" becomes aware of their absence and stops singing.)

ALICE: Why, they've gone! That was the strangest Tea Party I've ever been to! Now I know why it's called the March Hare; it certainly marched out of here! And who'd have thought that fractions could be part of making music? I'll look forward to learning them in school now. But first I have to get back to school. Everyone seems to be going to see the Queen. Perhaps I should too. Surely the Queen of Numberland will know the way for me to get out. Which way did the Math Hatter go? *(Audience tells her)* Oh, thank you! *(Heads off after Hatter)*

C.C. CAT: *(Head only appears in hole in back-screen)* Alice? Rats, just missed her. I have to tell her about the Queen. Maybe you cats can help me again? Here's a little trick question Alice will need to stop the Queen from taking her head off. It's "How do you square a circle?" Can you say that, everybody? "How do you square a circle?" One more time. "How do you square a circle?" When Alice asks for help, give her that. Everybody dig? Cool... *(Disappears)*

ALICE: *(Enters from opposite side of blackboard)* I've never met a Queen before. I suppose I should curtsy and... Oh! *(Produces Magician's bouquet)* What a beautiful garden. This must be the Queen's Summer Palace. I'd better put these back, though. I wouldn't want her Majesty to think...

QUEEN: *(Comes through door on screen in enormous, brightly-colored caftan)* Who dares to pick the royal flowers?

ALICE: Oh! Your Majesty. *(Curtsies, trying to stick flowers in desk at the same time)* I beg your pardon, but I truly wasn't picking the flowers. I was planting them.

QUEEN: Who dares to correct the Queen; especially with such poor logic! You don't plant flowers. You plant seeds. Make sense.

ALICE: I see what you mean. Well, I suppose I was re-planting them—although *these* never were seeds.

QUEEN: Absurd—you can have a seed without a flower, but not a flower without a seed. It's not logical. Use your head or lose it. What are you doing in the royal garden anyway?

ALICE: Your Majesty, I didn't mean to offend. I came to see if you might help me find my way out of Numberland.

QUEEN: Come closer, let me look at you. Hmmm— a little girl. Charming. Of course, you'll never find your way through Numberland, but I may keep you as a pet.

ALICE: Never find my way? But why?

QUEEN: Because girls and numbers don't mix. Everyone knows that.

ALICE: But I've learned that anyone can use numbers; girls, boys, carpenters, scientists, even musicians. And I don't want to be a pet. I want to think for myself.

QUEEN: *(Becoming angry)* So! You think you know all the answers?

ALICE: Well, no, but I do know that I should ask questions when I don't and...

QUEEN: You defy me again, little big head! I know how to get that head back down to size—Off with it!

ALICE: Off with what?

QUEEN: Off with her head! Soldiers, grab her.

33

(QUEEN whirls around, revealing three flashcard-bodied soldiers, painted on the back of her caftan. They advance menacingly.)

ALICE: *(Starts to run, then turns)* Why, I'm not afraid of you. You're just a pack of flashcards, and I know the answers. Two and Two, you're four; *(It collapses)* four and four, you're eight: *(It collapses)* eight and eight, you're sixteen. And sixteen and sixteen are...

QUEEN: *(Whirls to face Alice, furious. Speaks in a witch-like incantation)*
Don't tell me—I'm thirty-two.
Older, smarter far than you!
I know answers you don't know.
You cannot stump me and so
Unless you ask me a question I can't answer, (which I dread)
I will come and take your head!

ALICE: *(Hiding by the mushroom)* Oh, help me! Cheshire Cat! Anybody! *(To audience)* Is there any riddle she can't answer? (Audience answers: "How do you square a circle?") How do you square a circle?

QUEEN: *(Screams as if struck by acid)* No one has solved that, you wretched child! Not the greatest mathematicians, cleverest computers, no one yet! Oh my. *(Seems to shrink)* I feel a little faint. *(Begins to back offstage, frail and muttering)* How do you trisect an angle; I hate that! Fermat's last theorem,[1] oh, dear, oh, dear.

ALICE: Why, she wasn't such a monster after all. I guess no one knows all the answers. I wish she'd told me the answer to going home, though. Wait. Perhaps she did. The Queen said to use my head and be logical. Now, is it logical that I'm lost here in blackboard land? No—then I must still be in the classroom. *(Changes the blackboard to the classroom set)* And I am! So this must not be a giant mushroom at all—it must be my desk! *(Changes it to desk, hiding flowers in desk with same move)* And it is. And if this wasn't really Numberland, then it must be a dream—but how do I wake up? I know; please help me one last time. Call for my teacher, Mr. Dodgson. Just call, "Help, teacher."

(As audience begins to call, she puts her head on the desk. ACTOR enters as MR. DODGSON and goes to waken her)

MR. DODGSON: Alice, Alice—wake up. I'm sorry. I didn't realize how tired you were. Perhaps I shouldn't have kept you.

ALICE: Mr. Dodgson, it's all right. Look, *(Surprised to see it's true)* I've done all my problems. But there is one question I want to ask you.

MR. DODGSON: Why Alice, well done! Ask me anything you like.

ALICE: *(Sweetly)* How do you square a circle?

MR. DODGSON: Alice! However did you think of that? That's a question with no answer.

ALICE: Yet, Mr. Dodgson. But I may become the mathematician to answer it. *(Closes book, grabs her book bag, and skips off behind screen)*

MR. DODGSON: What an extraordinary child!

THE END

---

[1] Pierre de Fermat (1601-1665) was one of the developers of calculus and established the foundation of the theory of numbers. In the margin of his copy of Arithmetica, Fermat wrote: "It is impossible to divide a cube into two cubes, or a fourth power into two fourth powers, or in general any power ad infinitum into two like powers. I have found a rather marvelous proof of this, but the margin is too small to hold it." Fermat's proof was never found, and no mathematician has ever been able to offer a proof in its place.

GEORGE WASHINGTON CARVER: BORN TO SUCCEED

BY Bryan C. Reeder

© Bryan Reeder, 1988

Overdependence on cotton led to serious soil depletion in the South by the turn of the century. Through research and experimentation at the Tuskegee Institute, George Washington Carver (pictured above with a student) discovered that peanuts and sweet potatoes were well suited to Southern soil and could serve as profitable alternative crops.

PLAYWRIGHT'S NOTES

The one-act play "George Washington Carver: Born to Succeed" is an attempt to convey the spirit of determination that motivated one of America's greatest scientific minds. While it does detail Carver's major accomplishments, I hope that the play transcends an arid recitation of facts and dates. The play strives to illustrate Carver's resiliency in the face of the many obstacles that he encountered throughout his life.

Carver is truly one of the most amazing figures of modern history. In spite of the prejudice that he faced every day of his life, his humane spirit, quest for knowledge, and love of learning enabled him to rise above the prevalent attitudes and misconceptions of his day.

In a world where the more things change the more they stay the same, a role model of Carver's stature shows that zeal, drive, and dedication can and do make a difference in success.

A note about the casting: in the St. Louis Science Center production, one actor was used to play various people in Carver's life. This was accomplished through changing costume pieces. I believe that this method of casting is effective since it helps to convey the different attitudes that Carver confronted as well as portraying those who had an influence on his life.

The author wishes to thank Marsha Hollarder Parker for her invaluable help in researching Carver's life, John Banks who originated the role of Carver, and the entire staff of the St. Louis Science Center for their support of this work.

PRODUCTION HISTORY AND NOTES

In 1987, the St. Louis Science Center asked Bryan Reeder, director of theater at Lindenwood College in nearby St. Charles, to develop a short play to complement the ASTC traveling exhibition, *Send Us a Lady Physician*. The success of this play encouraged the Science Center to apply to the local Arts and Education Council for a grant to cover the costs of writing and producing a play on George Washington Carver in celebration of Black History Month in 1988. Bryan Reeder also served as director of the play and assisted with its production in 1989 as an outreach vehicle to schools.

In February 1988, 2,468 people saw "George Washington Carver." The play was produced nine times for school groups and five times for the general public in the 228-seat McDonnell Star

Theater at the St. Louis Science Center. During February and March 1989, the play was performed at 13 elementary and middle schools in the St. Louis region.

The Star Theater stage is only about 20 feet wide and 12 feet deep, has no curtains, and extends into the seating area; thus, the performance is virtually on top of the audience. The play was designed with this space in mind, and calls for few props, so that the theater could shift easily from the play to its regularly scheduled star shows.

Two actors and simple costumes are all that are needed; student actors were hired for a specific number of shows.

PRODUCTION RIGHTS

Contact the Education Department at St. Louis Science Center, 5050 Oakland Avenue, St. Louis, MO 63110; 314/289-4409.

GEORGE WASHINGTON CARVER: BORN TO SUCCEED

(An ACTOR, dressed as a SENATOR in 1865, enters. HE crosses center and addresses the audience.)

SENATOR: Let every man know that on this eleventh day of January, year of our Lord one thousand eight hundred and sixty-five, slavery is abolished in the State of Missouri, now and forever. None hereafter shall know any master but God.

(An elderly GEORGE WASHINGTON CARVER enters from the back of the house. HE and the SENATOR speak as one.)

GEORGE & ACTOR: The inalienable gift of song swells. A new spiritual is born which holds all joy, all sorrow, all yearning, all endeavor—the humility of man before his God. And the beginning and end is but one word. Free.

(ACTOR exits. GEORGE speaks directly to the audience.)

GEORGE: Free. I was five years old when those words were uttered. I was a slave at the time. What do you know about slavery? *(Response)* All that is correct, but the word "slave" is not quite enough to describe the relationship we had with the Carvers. The Carvers were a white couple who lived in Diamond Grove, Missouri. I never really knew my mama or my daddy. What I know of them comes from Uncle Moses Carver. He bought my mama, Mary, when she was thirteen years old. The Carvers were pioneering people and they were very much anti-slavery and were kindly folk. It may sound odd to you that someone who is against slavery would purchase another human being. There is something you need to understand about the Carvers. The simple fact is that they were middle-aged folk and building a home in the Missouri wilderness was too much for them to handle by themselves. They loved my mama and treated her like one of the family, not like a piece of property. While she was with the Carvers my mama met my daddy and she gave birth to my brother James and me.

When she was nineteen and I was just a baby, my mama and I were kidnapped by Kansas Raiders during the range wars between Kansas and Missouri. Uncle Moses hired a bushwacker to find mama and me. He found me, but I never saw my mama again.

(ACTOR steps on stage, wearing costume suggesting a bushwacker. HE carries a bundle wrapped in a blanket. Speaks to MOSES CARVER, who is at the back of the auditorium.)

BUSHWACKER: No sign o' Mary. First I heared she was dead, then somebody said they saw her goin' north with some soldier, and somebody else said she was sent down river to Louisiana. I guess them Kansas Raiders didn't want to be bothered with this baby. *(Pause)* No, I won't take the timberland you promised, since I couldn't get your girl. I'll just take your horse for my trouble. *(Extends arms)* The baby? Guess it's alive. *(exits with bundle)*

GEORGE: The Carvers took care of me until I was about ten years old. *(Looks into audience)* You know, you are really very fortunate. You get to go to school. When I was your age, the Missouri Constitution required that children attend school, but this did not apply to black children like me. But I was fortunate too because of Uncle Moses Carver. I told him that I wanted to learn and he was very understand-

41

ing. He sent me to the nearest school, about eight miles away. It was a small log cabin in which about seventy-five other children sat. Other than Uncle Moses, the person I remember best from my childhood is Mr. Foster, my first teacher.

(ACTOR enters as MR. FOSTER)

MR. FOSTER: *(Addresses the audience)* What do you think when you hear the name George Washington Carver? *(Responses)* That all may be true. Let me share with you what I think when people mention his name to me. I tell them that I remember him as a nice, pleasant, if somewhat small and sickly child. He was always curious about everything. He was especially interested in nature and anything that had to do with plants. His neighbors use to call him the plant doctor because he made house calls to care for folks' ailing flowers and vegetables.

Whenever he came across a sickly plant, he would take it to his secret garden where he'd care for it. He would always return it in full bloom. He never lost a patient. By the time he was thirteen, I had taught him everything I could and it was time for him to move on. And move on he did. He traveled with a family to Fort Scott, Kansas, where he hoped the weather would help him grow and make him feel less ill. George Washington Carver was the best student I ever had the pleasure of teaching. I knew he would amount to something. He was truly an inspiration. To be honest, George had many things going against him as he began his travel down the road of life: even though slavery had been abolished, lots of white folks still looked down on black people. And there was also the fact that George was ill a great deal of the time. But he did not let these things stand in his way. I have never seen such drive and interest and determination to succeed in one so young. I am proud to have been a small part of his growing up. *(Exits)*

GEORGE: Mr. Foster was one of my most pleasant memories from childhood. But not all my memories were so nice. When I went to Fort Scott, Kansas, I witnessed the most frightening event of my life. I saw for the first time the cruelty of man against his fellow man. I was in town one afternoon and saw a black man dragged from jail. He was being beaten to death and women and children snatched bits of the poor man as if they were grabbing for some sort of souvenir. The body was dragged to the town square where it was set alight. *(Pause. GEORGE calms down and addresses the audience)* I'm sorry. I can never recall that incident without feeling the same sense of horror. At daylight, I ran away from that god-forsaken place forever. Over the next few years, I moved from town to town, doing household chores and helping with harvest when my health would permit. People felt sorry for me and tried to give me handouts, but I wouldn't accept them. You see, I always preferred to work for my meals and shelters—things like that mean so much more when you earn them, don't they? But there were other people who did not feel sorry for me. In my travels, so many people tried to tell me that there were things that I could not do just because of the color of my skin.

(ACTOR enters, dressed as a wealthy PLANTER of the time)

PLANTER: Boy! When you're finished with what you're doin' for the missus, I want you to go out back to the woodshed and chop me some wood. *(Notices book)* Whoa, boy! What's this? *(Holds up book)* What in the blazes are you doing with this? *(Laughs)* Who ever heard of a black boy tryin' to read a book? Let me give you a piece of friendly advice, boy. You keep your place. Don't try to put yourself on the same level as your betters. You are different, boy, and don't you ever forget it. *(Exits)*

GEORGE: Of course I didn't listen to such nonsense. People like him are bullies—they try to make you act in a certain way because they don't understand who you are or what you are trying to accomplish. While things like this upset me a great deal, I refused to give up. If anything, it made me want to show these people that I could do anything I set my mind to. It made me want to learn as much as I possibly could. As I traveled from town to town, I attended school whenever I could. When I finally graduated from high school, I wanted to do something that very few black men had done up to that point. What do you think that was? I wanted to attend college. I continued to work and save all the money I could. I went to Highland University and fulfilled all the entrance requirements. I was almost accepted.

(ACTOR enters dressed as PRINCIPAL of Highland University)

PRINCIPAL: The most shortsighted thing I ever did as principal of Highland University was to turn down the application of one Mr. George Washington Carver. I remember looking over his application papers: a gifted young man, excellent grades in the schools he had attended. A talent for working with plants. He would be a fine addition to any school in this country. And then he came to see me. There was a knock at my door. *(GEORGE knocks)* What do you want?

GEORGE: I am George Washington Carver, sir. I've come to enroll in your school.

PRINCIPAL: We don't take coloreds here. *(Exits)*

GEORGE: If you've ever really wanted something more than anything else and did not get it for an unfair reason, then you might have some idea of how I felt at that moment. I had used all of my money to travel to Highland University and when they would not take me, I was flat broke. So, I had to stay there. Luckily, I was befriended by some very nice ladies from the Presbyterian church who were mighty upset over the way the university had treated me. I worked for the families of these ladies until I had saved enough money to buy a little tract of land in the western plains of Kansas. I lived on that land for four years, but it was barren and unproductive. No matter what I did, I couldn't make anything grow there. But I was able to grow personally. I discovered that I had a talent for painting, and all modesty aside, I wasn't too bad at it. Later on, I would always say that one of the major conflicts of my life was whether to devote my life to art or science. After my four years in Kansas, I traveled to Iowa. At last, I was able to fulfill my dream. In 1890, I entered Simpson College, mainly because they offered an art course. It wasn't easy at first, especially when it came to making money and friends, but eventually, I came to think of Simpson as home.

(ACTOR enters dressed as a college STUDENT of the time)

STUDENT: The first time I visited George in his room, I saw him stir a cauldron of boiling clothes—he did fellow students' laundry to make some extra money—take a bite of dinner and read a sentence in his textbook all at the same time. During the time I knew him, I learned that he could make lace, do carpentry work, and paint some of the most beautiful pictures of flowers that I had ever seen in my life. Everyone admired George. One of our teachers said that he was an excellent student with clear insight, determination, and great patience. He was more than a good student; he played on the baseball team, joined the literary society, helped to find music for school concerts, and was one of the four leaders of the local YMCA. He had many friends. One of these friends would change his life forever by getting him into the Iowa State College of Agriculture and Mechanical Arts. *(Exits)*

GEORGE: My years at the College of Agriculture were among the most exciting years of my life. I continued to paint, but I don't want you to think that all I did was paint. I studied. Oh my, did I study! I took courses in geology, chemistry, zoology, bacteriology, just about every "ology" you can think of. But my best subject was botany. Do you know what botany is? It is the study of plant life. I had always been interested in plants, and I made the decision to devote my life to the study of these wondrous creations. I worked very hard during the four years I was at the College of Agriculture and had the distinction of being the first black graduate of that institution. After graduation, I was offered a job—as a florist. Well, I gently told them "No, thank you."

Just between us, I did not earn my college degree so as to arrange flowers for dead people. And you know what? It turned out to be a wise decision because shortly after that, the College of Agriculture offered me a job—as a teacher! It was another first for both the College and me. Not only was I the first black to graduate from that school, but I was also the first black to teach there. I stayed at the College of Agriculture for about two years and then I met a man I'm sure most of you have heard of. How many of you have heard of Booker T. Washington? Well, Mr. Washington offered me a job on the staff at Tuskegee Institute in Alabama. At Tuskegee, I was trying to work out solutions to the problems that were facing the American farmers. You see there were two problems that faced the American farmer during that time: the one-crop system, which means that all the farmer planted was cotton, and simple human ignorance. To fight the one-crop system, I did a number of experiments to see which types of crops would grow best in Southern soil. To fight ignorance, I educated the people. You see, education is very important. Since most of the farmers could not come to me to learn of my findings, I brought my findings to the farmer.

(ACTOR enters dressed as a FARMER)

FARMER: There is a day I will never forget as long as I live. It was a day that changed not only my life, but the lives of my fellow farmers as well. It was May 24, 1906. I had gone into town to get a few supplies, when this wagon pulled into the town square. Can you guess who was on that wagon? That's right—it was Mr. George Washington

Carver! Quite a crowd gathered to hear what he had to say and what he said proved to be mighty important.

GEORGE: My friends, today I have come to talk to you and in talking together, we can help all of America—particularly her land. Let's be honest with one another. The Southern farmer is in a great deal of trouble. The Southern soil is just not as productive as it could be. The main problem facing you today is the one-crop system. For too long, the South has depended on only one crop: cotton.

FARMER: But Mr. Carver, all we've ever done is plant cotton. We've tried other crops, but none take to the soil as well. What else is there?

GEORGE: Sir, the South has depended on cotton because it is a cash crop. As I'm sure you know, when the cotton crop is poor, the Southern farmer is also poor. What we need is not to replace the cotton but to find some alternative to it—something to fall back on when the cotton crop is not as good as was expected.

FARMER: What kind of alternative, Mr. Carver?

GEORGE: There are several things. One of the best is this little bean that comes to us from China. Does anyone know what this is? It's a soybean. This miraculous little bean can do many wonderful things. Do any of you know what some of these things are? It is a valuable source of oil, and it can be used as hay. It grows best where there is a lot of moisture and the South certainly has plenty of that.

FARMER: Yeah? So?

GEORGE: So, soybeans are an important food for humans because they contain a great many proteins. Not only that, but soybeans can be sold to industries for very high prices. If you don't like soybeans, try sweet potatoes.

FARMER: You mean yams?

GEORGE: That's right. Everyday, ordinary yams. Yams, like soybeans, have numerous uses. They can be dried and ground and used as a coffee substitute. They can be grated and used as a starch. Syrup can be extracted from them. My friends, I have found no fewer than one hundred and eighteen uses for the sweet potato. I cannot stress how much good can come from a normal yam.

FARMER: This is really incredible, Mr. Carver. I never would have thought that a soybean or a sweet potato could be used in so many different ways. What else have you discovered?

GEORGE: The most exciting discoveries I have made come from the peanut.

FARMER: The peanut! You're pulling our legs, aren't you?

GEORGE: Not at all. Of all the vegetables on earth, the peanut is the most miraculous. Like the soybean, it can be used as hay, and the oil that is extracted from it can be used as cooking oil or for making shortening. It can be treated by a special process and used as a flour. Did you know you can make a type of glue from the peanut?

FARMER: Huh?

GEORGE: It's true. You can make peanut meal glue which is much stronger and works much better than normal plywood glues. Believe it or not, peanuts can be used to make certain types of paper. Come inside and let me show you some other things I have discovered...
(Exits behind screen)

FARMER: During that speech, Mr. George Washington Carver explained that there were as many as three hundred different ways that the peanut could be used. He was without a doubt one of the smartest men I ever heard. He not only told us about the need to change our planting habits, but our eating habits as well. He taught us how to cook the things he suggested we grow like the soybean and the peanut and how to preserve meat so that it could be used all year long. Mr. Carver was smart enough to realize that there was no use teaching us how to raise vegetables when we didn't know what to do with them. So he taught us how to pickle, can, and preserve. He also developed four new strains of cotton, called the Carver hybrid. Most normal cotton stalks produced only two bolls. The Carver hybrid produced two-hundred and seventy-five bolls. And they were by no means puny; they were huge. Later, he developed the Farmer's Institute. He taught us all manner of things: plantin', processin', animal care, butter-makin', even fire prevention. If it hadn't been for

Mr. Carver, I shudder to think what might have happened to the Southern farmer. Did you know that he not only helped people in his own country, but in other countries around the world? He traveled to Australia and helped them the same way he helped us. He was a friend to everyone, from poor, ordinary folks like me, to presidents and kings. It's hard to believe that a man who came from such humble beginnings could become one of the greatest Americans who ever lived. But he did. *(Exits)*

GEORGE: *(Reenters)* In spite of all my discoveries, I was never a rich man. I always preferred to have others make money off the results of my experiments. My work was not meant to make money for myself. I personally had very little use for money. I had always hoped to be able to do something for my people, and my work *did* help poor black farmers of the South. It also helped poor white farmers and these were my greatest rewards. My whole reason for living was to try and develop a greater respect between the races, based on my own effect on people. Looking back on my life, I think I can correctly state that I achieved that goal. Before I go, I have just one more thing to say to you: don't ever give up. You can be whatever you want, but you have to really want it and you have to really try. Challenge yourselves, listen to your teachers, and develop a curious attitude about this wonderful world we live in. Who knows, maybe one of you will grow up and continue in my footsteps helping people through science. Thank you for your attention. *(Exits)*

THE END

SARA
THE
SCIENTIST

BY Heidi Arneson

3

© Heidi Arneson and The Science Museum of Minnesota, 1985

Margo Andrews, Neil Spencer, and Joan Lisi debate which toys are appropriate for baby Sara in the Science Museum of Minnesota's production of "Sara the Scientist."

Neil Spencer and Joan Lisi compare Christmas presents in the Science Museum of Minnesota's production of "Sara the Scientist."

PRODUCTION HISTORY AND NOTES

"Sara the Scientist" is a short play consisting of a series of vignettes that follow the life of one woman from babyhood to adulthood. It was developed as a component of the *Women in Science and Engineering* exhibition, then on display at the Science Museum of Minnesota.

The first few scenes are principally comic, the last few more serious. There are moments of great poignancy in the play and it is important not to lose these in the interest of maintaining a fast pace.

"Sara" is a show requiring maximum cooperation, discipline, and timing. For the actress playing Sara it offers an opportunity to develop a character from childhood, through adolescence, to adulthood, all in a half-hour time span. For the actor and actress playing all the other roles, it offers a chance to put into play all of their characterization skills and techniques.

It is important to remember that Sara is telling a story—her story—during the play and therefore addresses the audience very directly throughout, not only in her opening and closing statements.

It is also important to keep in mind that we are addressing discrimination and stereotyping, so in those scenes where a stereotype is being spotlighted, mannerisms, expressions, and subtle power plays can strengthen that stereotype. For example, the male teacher's condescending smile, the father's attitude towards the mother, and the boyfriend's power play—in each of these scenes, the stereotype is at work all the time, not just in these footnoted key lines. Attention should also be given to the female supervisor who is supportive of a discriminatory system, and the husband who shares in all aspects of child care and supports Sara's career.

It is true that we have made great headway in reducing some of the overt discrimination against girls and women. All we need do, however, is turn on our television sets or open a women's magazine to realize that in our society a woman's appearance is more highly valued than her mental or spiritual qualities, and that a female's feelings of self worth are maintained only with ongoing and tremendous effort. Whether we want to devote our lives to motherhood or science, our choices will be assaulted. If we choose to do both, the road will be a rough and stony one. Sara seeks to point out some of the stonier places our choices will lead us to, while inspiring us to continue the work of easing the path for our daughters who will follow.

SET: Sara's box: a flat-topped, large box. Removable lid. A low stool. A low square table.

PROPS: All the props (except rag doll and baby blanket) can be cut and painted cardboard. The rag doll can be a simple, asexual caricature of actress playing Sara.

PROP LIST

The Toy Store
    1. rag doll
    2. baby blanket
    3. doll dress, pink and ruffled
    4. teddy bear
    5. children's baseball cap
    6. small doll
    7. blocks
    8. toy football
    9. toy airplane
    10. toy hammer
    11. baby bonnet, pink and ruffled
    12. toy gun

Bedtime Story
    1. baby blanket
    2. a doll (one that can be dismembered onstage and put together for the next show)

Kindergarten
    1. headband with question mark "antennae"
    2. picture of a scientist (for teacher's visual aid, large and colorful)

Christmas
    1. play dishes
    2. play chemistry set
    3. play broom and dustpan
    4. microscope
    5. play stove
    6. play rocket ship
    7. small tree with presents

Dress Up
1. Barbie doll
2. lipstick
3. two oversized, colorful bras

Math Class
1. books for each
2. a pencil for the teacher

Dissecting a Frog
1. frog dissection manual
2. pencil
3. two forks
4. two plates painted with supper
5. math book and paper
6. scalpel

Play Dumb
1. bone chart

Baby
1. rag doll wrapped in blanket
2. bottle

COSTUMES: Base costumes for all 3 actors: e.g., leotards & tights; pants/skirts and tops; one-piece outfits.
    Add-on costumes can be real: e.g., vests, jackets, skirts, etc,; or, as in SMM's production, cut-out stick-ons, like paper-doll costumes, attached at shoulders and waist with Velcro.

PRODUCTION RIGHTS

Contact Tessa Bridal, Theatre Department, Science Museum of Minnesota, 30 East 10th St., St. Paul, MN 55101; 612/221-4712.

SARA THE SCIENTIST

INTRODUCTION

(SARA enters. She stands, listening to the voices)

ACTOR: Women have a head too small for intellect, but big enough for love.

ACTRESS 1: Little girl! You would make a lovely model or cocktail waitress. But keep out of science! And leave math to the men!

ACTOR: Femininity is a congenital disease.

SARA: Those are the voices I heard as I grew up. My name is Sara. When I was a little girl, I dreamed of becoming a scientist. Did my dream come true? Or did I believe what the voices told me? We can look in the box and find out. *(Opens box, takes out baby)* Here I am as a baby. In the year 1948. What is the first thing I remember? My baby blocks. My father bought these for me. *(FATHER enters, takes baby)* The store clerk wore a bright dress, and an old woman wearing this hat toddled into the shop...

(BEGIN SCENE: TOY STORE)

CLERK: May I help you?

FATHER: Baby blocks?

CLERK: Right here. Boy or girl? Let me guess. A strong grip. Husky legs. A boy! Big and strong! Grow up and make lots of money.

(Enter WOMAN)

CLERK: May I help you?

WOMAN: A red truck?

CLERK: I'll look. *(CLERK disappears)*

WOMAN: Boy or girl?

55

FATHER: Girl.

WOMAN: I always wanted a girl, to dress up. Here's a pretty dress.

CLERK: *(Returns)* A red truck...Take that off! She looks ridiculous!!

WOMAN: The dress looks pretty!

CLERK: You want a truck!

WOMAN: A teddy bear.

CLERK: A baseball cap.

WOMAN: A dolly.

CLERK: An airplane...A football...

WOMAN: A bonnet!

CLERK: A hammer!

WOMAN: A dress!

CLERK: A gun!

FATHER: SHE WANTS THE BLOCKS!!!

CLERK: She? A girl? You little actress. Try the dress on. Pretty little thing.

FATHER: Just the blocks.

CLERK: Bye-bye, sweetie! Don't hurt yourself with the blocks!

(Other ACTORS freeze or exit)

SARA: I built worlds out of my blocks, then broke worlds apart, then began to take the REAL world apart... My blanket. My dolly. *(Removes them from box)* It's bedtime. In the darkness I hear Mother's heart beating...

(BEGIN SCENE: BEDTIME STORY)

MOTHER: Cinderella swept the floors and washed windows and beat rugs and baked bread and roasted pigs for her wicked family. All SHE ate was bread crust and dishwater. WHAT ARE YOU DOING?!

(SARA is dismembering her doll)

SARA: Where's her heart?

MOTHER: You took her apart!

SARA: Is she alive?

MOTHER: Howard!

(FATHER enters)

MOTHER: She's done it again. First the pillows, then the flashlight —

FATHER: The toaster —

MOTHER: The vacuum —

FATHER: The toilet tank —

MOTHER: The typewriter —

FATHER: Dead birds —

MOTHER: What next? The furnace? The television? She'll take everything apart.

SARA: I just want to see what's inside.

FATHER: NO MORE TAKING THINGS APART!

SARA: What about eggs and bananas and Christmas presents? *(Sucks thumb)*

FATHER: Good girls don't break things! *(Takes Sara's thumb out of her mouth)* Good girls keep their hands in their laps! *(SARA begins to ask a question)* Good girls don't ask questions!

(ACTORS Freeze or exit)

SARA: The day came when I had to leave my dolly home and go to school. I was petrified, but I was full of questions and my teacher let me ask them. She knew a lot of answers......*(JACK enters and chases her)* Jack!

(BEGIN SCENE: KINDERGARTEN)

TEACHER: This is a picture of a scientist.

SARA: What's a sniatiss?

TEACHER: Can you say scientist?

BOTH KIDS: Sci-en-tist.

TEACHER: A scientist is a man who asks questions about the world, then tries to find the answers to the questions he asks.

JACK: Like do fish have ears?

SARA: Like why is blood red?

JACK: Like why people die?

SARA: What makes things work? What makes a baby? What's inside things?

TEACHER: Yes.

SARA: I want to be a scientist.

JACK: Ha Ha! You can't be! YOU'RE A GIRL! GIRL GERMS!

(Other ACTORS freeze or exit)

SARA: I can't be a scientist? Why not? And what are girl germs? Can

I see them in a microscope? "Girl Germs." I heard that from my brother Peter, too. *(Tree is set with presents under it)* Peter, remember that Christmas Eve we ran through snow in our stocking feet? Mother, I remember your eggnog, and the packages reflecting the lights of the tree...

(BEGIN SCENE: CHRISTMAS)

PETER: What did Santa bring you?

SARA: I got a set of play dishes.

PETER: I got a chemistry set.

SARA: I got a broom and dustpan.

PETER: I got a microscope.

SARA: I got a stove.

PETER: I got a rocket ship.

SARA: Can I see your chemistry set?

PETER: No.

SARA: Can I see your microscope?

PETER: No.

SARA: Can I see your rocket ship?

PETER: No! Too dangerous for you!

SARA: You can play with my toys if I can play with–

PETER: I DON'T PLAY WITH GIRL STUFF!

SARA: Wish I'd got a microscope...*(Reaches for it)*

PETER: Let go of that!

SARA: I wanted a microscope!

PETER: Let go or I'll crush your fingers!

MOTHER: *(Enters)* Stop it! Really, children, and on Christmas Day too...

SARA: Mom, does Santa Claus know what we REALLY want?

MOTHER: Only you know what you REALLY want, Sara.

(Other ACTORS freeze or exit)

SARA: What did I really want? To look pretty? When Mother was away, my friend Mary and I would sneak into Mother's room. We opened her drawers and boxes. We transformed ourselves into red-lipped women. We wondered if our bodies would ever look like the body of my Barbie doll...

(BEGIN SCENE: DRESS UP)

SARA: I figured out Barbie's measurements. I multiplied each by seven: 39-23-33.

SARA AND MARY: We'll never make it.

MARY: Ladies walk with dictionaries on their heads.
Ladies pinch their fingertips to make them curve.
Ladies wear clean underwear and always carry a hanky.

SARA: When we suck in our cheeks, we look like ladies. If we suck in our cheeks and outline our eyes, keep our chins down, suck in our stomachs, push down our shoulders, stick out our chests, we look like pretty ladies.

MARY: *(They look at each other)* Uh uh. *(Exit or freeze)*

SARA: Could I look like a Barbie doll? No. Who can? But I could find the answers to my questions in books. In books about caves, insects, microscopes, magic, and numbers. NUMBERS fascinated me. I couldn't step into the same river twice because every moment another million water droplets entered the river and changed it. I couldn't stop a bird in mid-flight. A circle had no beginning and no end. How could I divide the universe into pieces small enough to understand? *With numbers.* With mathematics. I loved it. But math class made Mary turn pale and tremble and sweat...

(BEGIN SCENE: MATH CLASS)

MARY: I don't want to go in there! Let me hide in a locker 'til math is over!

SARA: Come on!

MARY: I'll never use it; I'll get married.

TEACHER: Before we begin, I want to announce the Math Contest on Friday. First prize is a tie clasp. Now. A clothing dealer tried to sell a coat cut in last year's style. He marked it down from $50 to $42.50. It didn't sell. He marked it down to $36.13. It still didn't sell. He marked it down again. This time it sold. Now, if the last markdown was consistent with the others, at what price did he finally sell the coat? Mary? At what price did he finally sell the coat?

MARY: Who did he sell it to? Did the man know it was out of style? If he wore it, would people laugh?

TEACHER: Mary thinks just like a girl. Look, Mary. Very simple. *(Does this very quickly)* 50 X 2 = 100. 42.50 X 2 = 85. 100 - 85 = 15. 15%! 42.50 X 15 = 637.5, carry the decimal makes $6.37 from 42.50, get $36.13. 15%! 36.13 X 15 =541.95, carry the decimal, round off to 5.41. Subtract 5.41 from $36.13. Get $30.72! Simple!

SARA: You go too fast! Slow down! Teach us!

(TEACHER exits or freezes)

MARY: Yeah! *(Exit or freeze)*

SARA: Teach us how to learn. Teach us how to ask questions. I had a science teacher who said...

MALE TEACHER: Never stop asking questions. When you are 94 years old, I hope you are still asking questions about the universe.

61

You won't always get an answer. But don't let that stop you from asking!

SARA: So I asked him, Where can I get a scalpel?

MALE TEACHER: What would you do with a scalpel?

SARA: I would dissect things. And he gave me a scalpel...

(BEGIN SCENE: DISSECTING A FROG)

MOTHER: Supper's ready, Sara!

SARA: To open the body cavity, first remove the skin...

MOTHER: Supper's ready!

SARA: Keep the frog moist. The heart may still be beating.

MOTHER: SARA! SUPPER!

SARA: The frog has neither diaphragm nor ribs.

MOTHER: SARA! Peter, get Sara!!

SARA: A female frog's body cavity may be filled with ripening eggs. This is a female.

PETER: *(Enters Sara's space)* Come eat. *(Reacts in disgust)* SARA'S CUTTING OPEN A FROG!

SARA: Be QUIET!

PETER: WITCHES WERE BURNED ALIVE FOR DOING THAT!

MOTHER: COME TO SUPPER THIS INSTANT! *(SARA and PETER arrive at table)* How was school?

PETER: I have a math problem.

MOTHER: Not for me!

SARA: Let me see it.

MOTHER: At lunch today I had to divide the tip. Had to use paper and pencil. My hands dripped sweat.

PETER: Women and math don't mix. Not in their genes.

MOTHER: Not true! I used to love it. Used to get A's. But in high school, I asked the teacher for help with a problem. She sent me to the board, said to stand there 'til I figured it out. How could I do it with thirty pairs of eyes on me? My face went red, my hands dripped sweat—I never asked a question in math again— *(Exits)*

SARA: I think I've got it...*(Hands PETER the napkin she's been using to work out the problem)*

PETER: Let me check. The answer's in the back, but we have to show how we got it. That's right! *(SARA grabs napkin back)* GIVE ME THAT!

SARA: I'll help with your math, if you help with the dishes.

PETER: You have a deal. *(Exits)*

SARA: He helped me with the dishes—I helped him with his math—until he got tired of the dishes. We made a new deal: I did all his math—he gave me his microscope. I remember the night my first boyfriend came to study bones. He saw my microscope and called me "Dr. Frankenstein."

(BEGIN SCENE: PLAY DUMB)

FATHER: I'm home!

MOTHER: Hi, dear. Sara just had her boyfriend over. Studying anatomy. You should have seen them. Sara knew every bone. Show him, Sara.

SARA: *(With Chart)* Phalanges, Metacarpus. Carpus. Radius. Ulna. Humerus. Clavicle. Scapula. Ilium. Ischium. Pubis...

MOTHER: He only knew one. The humerus. Poor kid. *(Exits)*

SARA: He's cute!

FATHER: Come here, Sara. Do you want to keep your boyfriend?

SARA: Yes.

FATHER: Then don't act so smart. Men don't marry women smarter than they are. *(Exits)*

SARA: My high school counselor said:

ACTRESS 1: Science is a hard road for girls.

SARA: Said I was bright enough to be a high school biology teacher, but I wanted to be a scientist. So she sent me to an old woman who had worked in scientific research...

(BEGIN SCENE: THE OLD SCIENTIST)

OLD SCIENTIST: So you want to be a scientist, Sara? You are lucky to be alive today. Brave women paved the path for you. Women who worked in obscurity and isolation. Sophie Germain was a girl in the 18th century. She studied calculus in her room at night. Her parents were afraid this would damage her brain. So in the middle of the winter, they took away her firewood and candles to stop her from studying. But they couldn't stop her. She had a candle hidden away. She wrapped herself in quilts. She kept on studying. In the morning they found her asleep on her books, nails blue with cold, ink frozen, calculations covering her slate. She taught herself differential calculus. She became a great mathematician. They used to say if a woman used her brain too much, it would rob her womb of life force: "If you study you will give birth to small-brained men."

SARA: I've dated some of them.

OLD SCIENTIST: I had a hard time getting in. My interviews. I remember them well...

MALE VOICE: *(Establishes this pattern and repeats it several times as scientist talks)* We regret to inform you that we are unable to accept applications from women. We regret to inform you...

SCIENTIST: I heard that over and over until it repeated itself in my head as I tried to sleep. *(VOICE stops)* I finally got a job. Because of the war. I loved the test tubes, the petri dishes, the meticulous experiments. Even if the results belonged to someone else. Sometimes I worked until morning. I went home to an empty house. Nothing was in my head but the work. Listen. You've got to love it. Does it make your heart beat faster? You must come to know the bit of universe you study more clearly than you know the hand you write with. Science is infinite. It will put you in awe of this universe of which you are an infinitesimal part.

(Other ACTORS Freeze or exit)

SARA: If a girl could hide a candle away and study by its light in the frozen winter night until ice formed in her ink well, I could do it! I went to college to study... There I fell deeper in love with the microscope and deeper in love with the boy who called me "Dr. Frankenstein"....

(BEGIN SCENE: THE BROKEN HEART)

BOYFRIEND: Sara! Where were you last night?

SARA: David! I was in the lab.

BOYFRIEND: All night?

SARA: Do you know why eggs form little strings when you scramble them?

BOYFRIEND: No.

SARA: I was in the kitchen. Scrambling eggs. Suddenly, everything I've learned came together, I saw the biochemistry of scrambled eggs. I had to run to the lab and look through the microscope.

BOYFRIEND: We had a date.

SARA: I forgot.

BOYFRIEND: You forgot?! It'll only get worse when you finish school and get a job. Where will you get a job? Some other state? Think I'll follow you there? To do what? Sit alone all night while you look at a microscope? Quit school and I'll marry you.

SARA: I can't quit. You can't ask me that.

BOYFRIEND: I can't? Okay, then I can't stay. Good-bye, Dr. Frankenstein. *(Exits)*

SARA: Good-bye. Didn't my Father warn me? "Play dumb." But I didn't play dumb, and I didn't stop studying. I went on to graduate school and eventually I met another man who loved science as much as I did. We brainstormed together on the mysteries of microbiology. Eventually we were married....

(BEGIN SCENE: NEPOTISM RULE)

SARA: I married Paul because he was a scientist and we could work together. And now you tell me I am going to lose my job because I married him?

SUPERIOR: It's the RULE, Sara. The Nepotism Rule: two members of the same family cannot be employed in this institution. Generally it's a good rule. It keeps a man from handing out jobs to his sons and nephews. It's the rule.

SARA: So my husband stays on and I am forced to find another job. Probably out of state. And carry on a long-distance marriage.

SUPERIOR: Well, you could accept a position of assistant to your husband. Keep working beside him in the lab. No pay of course.

SARA: Of course. No pay and no OFFICIAL position.

SUPERIOR: Sorry, Sara. It's the Nepotism Rule. What can I do?

SARA: What could she do? What did I do? I took on an important job that required my strength and patience and imagination...24 hours a day, 7 days a week. A job that surprised me every morning, exhausted me every night, and rearranged everything in my life...Motherhood. With science I ask questions about life; but with motherhood I hold life in my arms and help it to grow...

(BEGIN SCENE: BABY)

(Baby crying, SARA and husband, PAUL, in bed)

SARA: What time is it?

PAUL: 3 A.M. I'll get the bottle. Is she wet?

(PAUL gets bottle, SARA gets Baby)

SARA: She's dry. Small and warm.

PAUL: Tiny and perfect.

SARA: Bright eyes.

PAUL: I can't keep my eyes off her.

SARA: I can't keep my eyes open.

PAUL: I'll take her.

(PAUL sings lullaby, SARA joins until she falls asleep)

PAUL: What are you going to be, little girl? Maybe someday you'll fly a rocket ship to Saturn. Or serve coffee in a restaurant. Just be happy.

SARA: We never realized how much work a baby would be: diapers, spit up, sleepless nights... My hair wasn't combed, Paul had purple circles under his eyes, and the kitchen floor was sticky, but we were parents AND scientists!

(PAUL exits)

SARA: I had stayed on as my husband's unpaid assistant in the lab; only when he moved on to a professorship with high pay and tenure was I again paid for my work. My hand adjusted the same fine focus knob of the same microscope in the same lab over one million times.

(BEGIN SCENE: THE RESEARCH ASSISTANT TRAP)

SUPERIOR: I hope you are not suggesting that we have discriminated against you, Sara.

SARA: I am saying that I have been a research assistant here for seven years. The men who came from below me have moved above me. I've stayed in the same place. My work is as good, if not better—

SUPERIOR: That's why we keep you here. What would we do without you?

SARA: You'd find someone to replace me.

SUPERIOR: This job is ideal for a mother. You don't have to go to meetings, you don't have administrative responsibilities, you don't have to teach classes. You are free to do the research that you love. What are you complaining about?

SARA: That's right. I follow instructions. I'm not allowed to control the lab. I never hear what the scientists in charge think about the work. Never get to discuss ideas with them. I can't expand. No responsibility. No recognition. Here is an example. I did the major work on the paper we just finished. Correct?

SUPERIOR: Yes.

SARA: And where is my name on the paper? At the bottom. Whose name is at the top?

SUPERIOR: Well, Sara, he is head of the lab.

SARA: Yes, and that's the way it is when you're a Research Assistant. You don't get credit for your work. And where do most women in science end up? In Research Assistantships!

SUPERIOR: The days of discrimination of women in science are over!

SARA: Who controls the funding? Who holds the positions of power? Men. We let women into the lower ranks and then leave them there.

SUPERIOR: I thought you were happy here.

SARA: I was! But I'm growing out of the job. If you don't move me up, I've got to move on.

SUPERIOR: Good luck, Sara. *(Exits)*

SARA: I had good luck. No, I had persistence. I looked and looked until I found another job with responsibility and room to grow. I feel at home in science now. Only 12% of our scientists in America today are women. I fought to make my dreams come true. What are your dreams? A young woman today can become almost anything she dreams of. Today it is against the law in this country to discriminate against a person because of age, color, or sex. But there are still voices. Silent voices that say...

MAN: Girls haven't got the brains.

OTHER WOMAN: They haven't got what it takes.

SARA: And there are new loud voices that shout:

MAN AND WOMAN: Women can and MUST have it all.

SARA: An education, a career, marriage...

MAN: Children...

WOMAN: A clean house...

MAN: Community involvement...

WOMAN: A slim body...

MAN: A beautiful face...

WOMAN: And straight white teeth...

BOTH: In a big pink smile!

SARA: It's confusing! What voice shall you listen to? Listen to the voice within yourself. You have what it takes to become what you dream of. It's inside you. And no one can take it from you.

THE END

BIBLIOGRAPHY

Brush, Lorelei R. *Encouraging Girls in Mathematics: The Problem and the Solution*. (Cambridge, Massachusetts: ABT Books Ass. Inc., 1980).

Donnelly, Patricia J., and George A. Wistreich. *Lab Manual for Anatomy and Physiology*. (New York: Harper and Row, 1982).

Fins, Alice. *Women in Science*. (Lincolnwood, Illinois: VGM Career Horizons, National Textbook Company, 1983).

Gleasner, Diana C. *Breakthrough: Women in Science*. (New York: Walker and Company, 1983).

Gornick, Vivian, ed. *Women in Science: Portraits from a World in Transition*. (New York: Simon and Schuster, 1983).

Hubbard, Ruth, Mary Sue Henifin, and Barbara Fried, editors. *Women Look at Biology Looking at Women*. (Boston, Massachusetts: Schenkman Publishing Company, 1979).

Kovalevskaya, Sofya. *A Russian Childhood*. (New York: Springer-Verlag, 1978.)

Lipsitz, Joan. "The Economic Future of Girls and Young Women." Keynote speech at conference on the Economic Future of Girls and Young Women. Wayzata, Minnesota, 1984.

Noble, Iris. *Contemporary Women Scientists of America*. (Englewood Cliffs, New Jersey: Julian Messner Publ., 1979).

Perl, Teri. *Math Equals: Biographies of Women Mathematicians*. (Reading, Massachusetts: Addison-Wesley Publishing Company, 1978).

St. Paul Pioneer Press and Dispatch, Friday, July 5, 1985.

Tobias, Sheila. *Overcoming Math Anxiety*. (New York: W. W. Norton and Company, Incorporated, 1978).

THE SOAP OPERA

BY Lincoln Bergman and
Barbara Ando,
Sylvia Branzei,
Mike Carbone,
Gigi Dornfest,
Randall Fastabend,
Anne Raftery, and
Marilyn Smith

© The Regents of the University of California, 1989

Rachel Glass as "Dr. Tallow and Mr. Tyde" in "The Soap Opera."

Opposite, top: David Quicksall (l), Linda Montalvo (m), and Sean Terry (r) as Al B. Grease, Soponia Handlebar, and Walter Waters in "The Soap Opera."

Opposite, bottom: Sean Terry (l) and Rachel Glass (r) play "Drawing Molecules for Laundry Money" in "The Soap Opera."

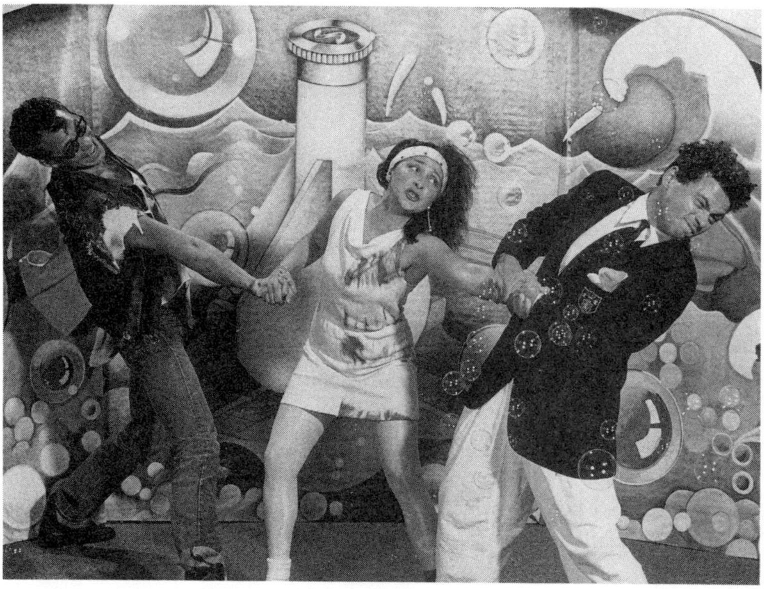

Richard Hoyt

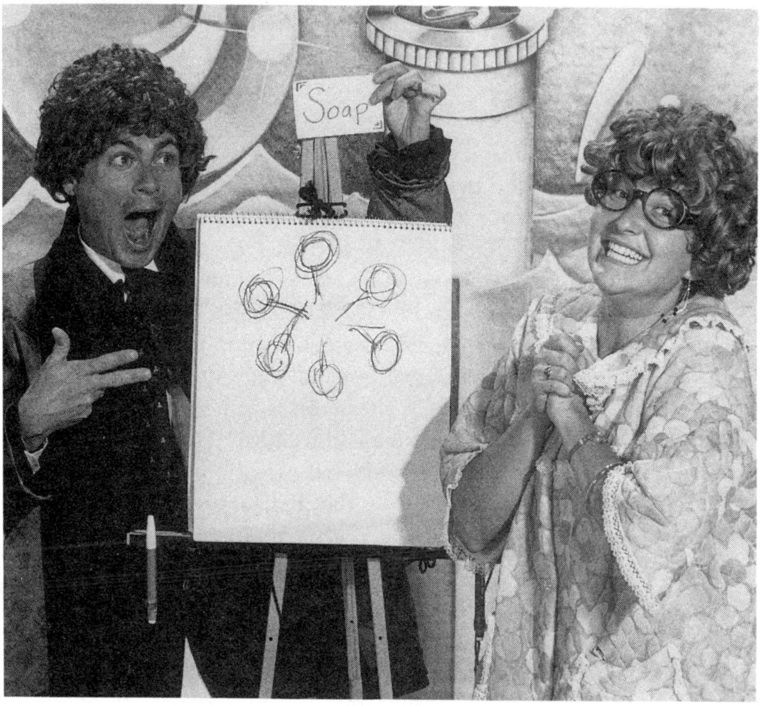

Richard Hoyt

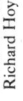

PLAYWRIGHT'S NOTES

The development and scriptwriting process for "The Soap Opera," as for all Science Discovery Theatre productions, was a group effort. Jacqueline Barber, director of chemistry at the Lawrence Hall of Science and author of the popular teacher's guide, Bubble-ology, had the initial inspiration to combine the melodramatic motifs of a TV soap opera with information about the chemistry of soap. The script committee (Barabara Ando, Lincoln Bergman, Sylvia Branzei, Mike Carbone, Gigi Dornfest, Randall Fastabend, Anne Raftery, and Marilyn Smith) included science educators, staff writers, the two co-directors of the production, and other staff members with expertise in the daily soaps or light opera.

Through library research, talks with LHS chemistry instructors, and hands-on experimenting, we explored how soap works. Freewheeling brainstorm gatherings evolved into more focused improvisational and preliminary script-reading sessions. A fine balance among science content, audience involvement, and entertainment was sought. Our initial goal was to convey how soap works within a soap opera/light opera framework. Our target audience was the middle school/junior high age group, but, like all Science Discovery Theatre Productions, the play, for performance at Lawrence Hall of Science as well as schools, needed to have interest and appeal for all ages.

Early discussions generated a fairly clear sense of basic plot—a classic triangle involving three characters representing the molecules of soap, water, and grease. In time, names emerged: Saponia Handlebar, Walter Waters, and Al B. Grease. Other characters soon bubbled up— an old-fashioned, radio-style Announcer and Saponia's kindly old Aunt Bubbles, a noted "Bubble-ologist." Commercials and brief messages were interspersed between scenes, many of them conveying science content in a direct, fast-moving way.

The choice of three main characters meant an "executive" (read budgetary) decision that we could use three actors at each performance. Previous productions had used two. There were clever ways we might have found to devise the play for only two, but in order to graphically demonstrate the actual molecular relationships, it was far better to be able to show the interaction between each pair and all three at the same time. Once we had the go-ahead on three actors we were off and spinning. It is worth noting that this limitation to three actors, when there are also a large number of minor roles, meant quick costume changes and increased audience amusement

74

when the same actor played widely disparate roles.

Numerous scripts were written and critiqued, various directions explored. Loads of words and scenes had to be washed down the drain, including much of the original light opera concept. Members of the committee worked in a truly collective playwrighting fashion, with key scenes, clever twists, and outstanding problem-solving skills contributed by all. Given our past experience, we knew that deciding upon one main theme to communicate was essential to effective educational and dramatic impact.

We agreed to limit the content to the way the two-sided nature of the soap molecule contributes to the cleaning process. While surface tension is mentioned in the play, a fuller discussion of it was considered and rejected in the same way we also chose not to focus on the distinction between soap and detergent, and the pollution problems that have been caused by various detergent formulations. These subjects and others are, however, discussed in the follow-up activity packet that accompanies school performances.

Toward the end of the script development process, the directors and several actors from previous productions did a read-through with some basic blocking. They were unanimous in concluding that the dramatic impact and science content were cleverly interwoven, and that the play was challenging, with great opportunities for actor creativity.

Auditions were held, and five actors were hired to alternate in the three main roles, depending on schedule. The Walter Waters character would also play The Announcer, while (hilariously, as it turned out) the Al B. Grease character would also play Aunt Bubbles. The two directors, Gigi Dornfest and Randall Fastabend, and the actors—Paul Codiga, Rachel Glass, Linda Montalvo, David Quicksall, and Sean Terry—made numerous refinements, truly bringing the characters and the entire production to life. A colorful set designed by Scarlen Manning and built by Victor Candia conveys the sense that the action takes place inside a giant washing machine. An amplified keyboard enhances the music and sound effects, and a real bubble machine launches hundreds of bubbles onto the stage at appropriate moments.

In the end, the molecular action of the soap molecule is demonstrated through a dramatic rescue scene and the three main character/molecules sum up the essential chemistry in their final song. A preview performance for staff, whose critique formed the final stage in the development process, was very well received, and "The Soap Opera" premiered in June 1989. Since then, it has played to enthusiastic audiences at the Lawrence Hall of Science and in schools all over the Bay Area. Although its science content and language are aimed at the middle school age group, it holds the attention of younger students, and adults find it amusing and challenging as well. Performances at schools include pre- and post-tests on science content as well as follow-up activities that teachers can use to extend the learning experience after the play has catalyzed interest.

PRODUCTION NOTES

The following notes from the first production of "The Soap Opera" are intended only as a guide. Directors of subsequent productions should feel free to experiment as their creativity leads them. We would be interested to hear of alternative "solutions" to the "Soap" adventure.

Since the play was written to be performed by three actors, they should be versatile, with the ability to change characterizations quickly. Each actor plays several roles, differentiating them through physical characterizations and costumes. For example, the actor playing the Announcer may wear glasses and remove them to become Walter. Al B. Grease may don a wig, granny glasses, and a large, colorful muumuu, becoming Aunt Bubbles. The breakdown of character assignments we used were:

1. Announcer/Walter/Rick Slick
2. Clem S. Tree/Al B. Grease/Aunt Bubbles
3. Saponia/Ester Bond/Dr. Tallow-Mr. Tyde/Elvis Permanent Pressley

The entire show was performed without a stage manager. The actors did all the pre-show set up, take down, props, and costume maintenance.

Actors should take time to develop characters past the "cartoon" stage. With the simple plot and short scenes in "The Soap Opera," it might be tempting for actors to oversimplify relationships and character development, but audience sympathy can be lost when the characters become too superficial. Hence, Aunt Bubbles would be funny performed as a Monty Pythonesque female impersonator, but such a caricature might be likely to detract from the science content she is meant to teach. There are also issues of sexism to be examined with such a choice.

The chemical relationship between the characters is underscored by their physical juxtaposition on stage. The actor playing

Walter typically enters and exits stage right. This position corresponds to the water-attracting side of Saponia. Al B. Grease enters and exits stage left, which represents Saponia's grease-attracting side. Saponia, taking center stage, is physically torn between her two "attractions."

Certain props may require additional explanation.
- Announcer's Cart contains an electronic keyboard, cassette player, microphone, and sound system. A cloth cover with the "As the Soap Churns" logo conceals the contents of the cart.
- Aunt Bubble's Cart is filled with an intriguing assortment of colorful bubble-making apparati. The character actually creates bubbles onstage (practice ahead of time with the fancy stuff!!).
- The Bubble Machine is an optional addition that is turned on by Aunt Bubbles before she goes on stage and shut off when she exits. Check with your local theatrical supplier for bulk supples of "bubble juice," and for the machine. We strongly advise that you experiment with different ratios of glycerin, soap, and water for optimal effects and minimal clean-up. We kept a towel backstage to catch "dribbles" and a carpet runner on that side of the stage to secure footing. (Soap can be slippery stuff!)
- Elvis Permanent Pressley, The King of Wash and Wear. We toyed with the idea of an actor playing Elvis, but settled on a life-sized cutout, recognizable as a "permanently pressed," flattened figure. An actor held up "Elvis" and sang his lines into the Announcer's microphone.

Taped theme music was used on a two-minute loop, making the job of the Announcer easier. An electronic keyboard was used for music chords, rhythms, and sound effects. The Announcer can use the keyboard effects to highlight the commercials and transitions between scenes. Al B. Grease's rap and the "rhyme fight" were accompanied by rhythms programmed on the keyboard.

The pacing of "The Soap Opera" is very brisk, but the speed should never act to the detriment of content. The quick changes, especially the commercial breaks, are intended to reinforce the content introduced during the "drama" without appearing repetitive. The audience should never feel rushed or overloaded by information, but instead involved in the plot and by the teaching the actors provide.

Evaluations of "The Soap Opera" from a variety of museum and school audiences indicate younger children (up to about second grade) are most attracted by the play's colorful visuals (bubble making), quick pacing and slapstick humor. Older children (through preteens) are drawn to the characterizations and the relationships, especially those of Saponia and Al B. Grease. Adults respond to puns and to the character of Aunt Bubbles. In the illustrious tradition of Rocky and Bullwinkle, "The Soap Opera" is intended to teach and appeal to a wide audience.

PROPS/TECHNICAL LIST

1. Tool box for set maintenance
2. "Applause" sign
3. Toy siren
4. Announcer's cart, with:
    electronic keyboard
    tape deck and cassettes (if used)
    two speakers
    amplifier
    microphone and stand
5. Aunt Bubble's cart, with:
    bubble solution
    variety of bubble-making apparati
    soap-making tray with measuring cup, labeled "Fatty Acid;" cup labeled "Base;" bar of soap, and mixing jar/bowl

Dr. Tallow Scene:
1. Covered coffee can labeled "Caustic Soda" on one side, "Grease" on the other
2. Cardboard Elvis Permanent Pressley figure

Game show scene:
1. large tablet or dry erase board
2. pens
3. cue cards

Washquake scene:
1. Oversized box labeled "SOAP"

PRODUCTION RIGHTS

For information on obtaining performance rights, or for scripts of other productions of the Science Discovery Theatre, contact Barbara Ando, Lawrence Hall of Science, University of California, Berkeley, CA 94720; 415/642-2858.

THE SOAP OPERA

SAPONIA HANDLEBAR: Saponia represents Soap. She is a powerful personality, very charismatic, attractive to different types of people. She has a "split personality" in the sense that part of her is drawn to water, but the other part is repelled by water and attracted to grease. This basic schizophrenia, however, is a strength, NOT a weakness, because it allows her to have power and control and lead the rescue in the end. She might be dressed in a two-tone costume, maybe grey/cream, and use physical movements and a right hand/left hand differentiation to represent being attracted and repelled to other two main characters, almost like magnetic attraction and repulsion. Her hair could be quite different on each side.

WALTER WATERS: Walter represents Water. He is a sophisticated, charming man, with very smooth and flowing movements, a continental or Maurice Chevalier type of grace, etiquette, etc. However, he overdoes it to the point of boredom. May fuss with large white handkerchief from time to time. Always exits and enters stage right.

AL B. GREASE: Stands for Grease. Al B. is a more proletarian sort, a streetwise rapper and auto mechanic whose roughness, daring, irreverence, and lack of concern for social niceties makes him very attractive to the side of Saponia that is attracted to grease. He could make motions as if he were constantly sticky and/or could have dirty clothes, etc. Has a dirty grease rag he uses as a handkerchief. Enters and exits stage left.

AUNT BUBBLES: Aunt Bubbles is Saponia's advisor, mentor, teacher, therapist, confidante. She is the one Saponia takes her troubles to, and is always ready with sage advice. She is also a "Bubbleologist" and throughout her appearance on the stage is experimenting with various bubble makers. Whenever Aunt Bubbles is on stage, an offstage bubble machine spews bubbles on stage.

THE ANNOUNCER: The Announcer is a caricature of an emcee or old-time radio announcer. Could also have attributes of a modern TV talk show host and circulate in the audience as noted below. Wears glasses. The microphone/keyboard panel is stage right.

BASIC CHEMISTRY: The cleaning action of soap involves the breaking up of oils and grease that bind dirt to clothes, skin, or dishes. A soap molecule has one end that is attracted to water and one end that is repelled by water and attracted to grease. When a greasy plate is washed with soapy water, the soap molecules attach to the grease with one end, with their water-attracting end still in the water. When the plate is rubbed with a sponge, the water pulls on the water-attracting end of the soap molecule, which in turn pulls on the grease attached to the other end. When the grease is pulled free of the plate, the soap molecules surround it, and it can be washed away with the water. Soap also decreases the surface tension of water to about one-third that of plain water. One consequence of this is the creation of suds and bubbles. Decreasing surface tension lessens the "stickiness" of water, making it "wetter" and more able to interact with oily, greasy, or waxy surfaces. The shape of a soap molecule is often compared to a lollipop, with the grease-attracting end being the "stick" and the water-attracting end the round candy.

SET: The set suggests the inside of a giant washing machine. A keyboard is set up to act as an organ, with an old-time radio microphone visible.
    The announcer combines echoes of TV soap operas with the style of an old-time radio show. ANNOUNCER warms up audience, circulating, asking where people come from, things about soap, implying that set is a washing machine, etc. As play begins the ANNOUNCER goes to keyboard, and begins dramatic, emotional theme music. After initial seconds of music, ANNOUNCER begins to speak in typically melodramatic soap opera style. ANNOUNCER speaks over music. (Or, alternatively, taped music can be used.)

ANNOUNCER: Welcome to the stirring saga that uncovers the wild world of chemical experience. Come with us now as we explore the attractions and reactions whirling within the washing machine in the never-ending battle against grime on "As the Soap Churns." *(Music off)* But first, a word from our sponsor.

ADVERTISEMENT #1 (NECKLACE)

MAN: *(In flashy suit/tie or garish cowboy outfit)* Hi, kids, I'm Clem S. Tree, from the Necklace Center. Do you have a credit problem? Do you never get credit for anything? Come down to the Necklace Center and we'll string a line of credit around your throat. Molecule necklaces, ionic bracelets, you name the element, we'll provide its atomic weight. Remember, ask for Clem S. Tree, at the Necklace Center. Bye kids. *(Items he advertises hang from inside his jacket, like stereotypical watch salesman)*

ANNOUNCER: *(Music)* In our last episode, the relationship between Saponia Handlebar and her boyfriend, Walter Waters, was sinking to a new low. Meanwhile, Al B. Grease, a local grease monkey and wanna-be rock star, is scheming on Saponia. But that's getting ahead of our story. As we rejoin our program, Saponia *(ENTERS, curtsies to audience, freezes)* who has just had another argument with Walter Waters, has gone to get some advice and have a heart-to-heart talk with her kindly Aunt Bubbles. Unfortunately Aunt Bubbles is not at home. Meanwhile, Walter Waters has followed Saponia to Aunt Bubble's house. *(Music off, ANNOUNCER takes off glasses and jumps into scene as WALTER WATERS).*

SCENE I

Living room of Aunt Bubbles' home. Bubble apparatus on cart stage left, also bubble machine. Enter WALTER WATERS from stage right. It's obvious he and SAPONIA have just had an argument.

WALTER: Saponia...

SAPONIA: Oh Walter, go away!

WALTER: Just tell me if it's true: have you been seeing someone else?

SAPONIA: Would it make any difference to you?

WALTER: Well, yes, I mean, no, I mean yes! I mean...

SAPONIA: Walter Waters, you're so wishy-washy. You're so...so...watered down! Where's the excitement, the adventure, the passion?

WALTER: *(Condescendingly)* Now Saponia, calm down. How about going for a watercress salad at the Cleanspot Cafe?

SAPONIA: *(Sarcastic)* The Clean Spot! How exciting. Walter, I'm not sure I want to hang out with you anymore.

WALTER: Saponia, you can't mean that. You know how I feel about you.

SAPONIA: *(Angrier)* Do I? Sometimes I wonder if you're even capable of feeling.

WALTER: Well, I...

SAPONIA: You'd better have a lot more to say for yourself than that, or we'll be..... we'll be.... ALL WASHED UP!

(Enter AL B. GREASE from stage left)

AL B.: *(Croons)* Saponia, baby.

SAPONIA: What are you doing here?

AL B.: Lookin' for you. Who's the wet blanket? *(Indicating WALTER, who's pouting)* Why don't we ditch this drip down the drain and do some dirty dancing? There's a band playing down at the Lint Trap club that'll clog your carburetor! The Slime Survivors.

WALTER: *(Shudders)* Oh...did he say "slime..." you know I can't stand to hear obscenities like that! *(To Al B.)* They should wash your mouth out with soap! *(To audience)* I prefer the Bleach Boys myself.

AL B.: Yeh, I said....SLIME! Wanta make something of it? *(Shouting at WALTER, who backs up each time a word is shouted)* Dirt! Mud! Crud! Grunge! *(Comes up next to Saponia)* I couldn't stop thinking about you, baby, since last week when I changed the oil in your car. Someone told me you hang around here at your Aunt's and I thought I might run into you. Look's like my timing's just right. What say we split this scene and party down!

SAPONIA: I couldn't possibly go out with you; I don't even know your name.

AL B.: Al B. Grease, at your service.

> Yeh, my name is Grease, and I can rap
> Don't like my song? Better shut your trap.
> Cause I'm strong and tough and rough enough
> To cover your clothes with grimy stuff
> No one removes my sludgy stain
> No one washes me down the drain.
> Yeh, my name is Grease and I am bad
> The biggest baddest dirt you've ever had.
> So if ya don't like the grease get outta the kitchen.
> If ya don't get dirty then you ain't livin'.
> If ya don't like my song, better shut your trap.
> My name is Grease and I can rap.

(SAPONIA starts to get into it, but WALTER glares at her)

AL B.: *(To SAPONIA)* You can call me AL B., or call me whenever you need me. *(A la Groucho)*

WALTER: *(Increasingly jealous but still at a distance)* How dare you talk like that to my little dew drop?

AL B.: *(To SAPONIA)* You're spendin' time with this liquid loser? I guess I came along *(Sings)* "Just in Time, You Found Grease Just in Time."

SAPONIA: (Uncomfortable) Walter and I were just going out for a watercress salad at the Cleanspot.

WALTER: Yes, and a glass of spring water!

AL B.: (Disparagingly) The Cleanspot! Hey, the Lint Trap has the best greaseburgers in town.

SAPONIA: *(Interested)* Really? I've never had a greaseburger.

AL B.: Yeah, and it's just right for a cozy chat and some slo-o-ow dancing. I'm off work at eight. Then let's you and me go agitate.

SAPONIA: *(Shudders with excitement)* The Lint Trap, a greaseburger, sounds great!

WALTER: I warn you Saponia, this time you're going too far!

SAPONIA: *(Pleased)* Why Walter, I think you're jealous!

AL B.: That's the spirit, Saponia. I'll see you later, then we'll come alive, and that's no jive! *(Exits stage left; doesn't slip on soap)*

SAPONIA: Seeya later, agitator.

WALTER: You'd better think this over. This is no time for your childish games. *(Exits)*

SAPONIA: See if I care! I'm old enough to live my own life! I don't want to lose Walter, but... I feel like I'm being torn in two. What's come over me? Aunt Bubbles, where are you? *(Runs off stage right)*

ANNOUNCER: *(Music)* Will slick, slippery Saponia lose reliable, rich, incredibly good-looking Walter Waters? *(Winks to audience)* Who is this Al B. Grease—what is it about him? Will Aunt Bubbles be able to tell her more? Where will Saponia wind up—at the brightly lighted Cleanspot Cafe or the dark, shadowy Lint Trap? Answers to these and other "pressing" questions when "As The Soap Churns" returns in a moment. *(Music out)*

ADVERTISEMENT #2 *(RICK & ESTER)*

ANNOUNCER: *(Changes into gameshow host coat and wig)* Be sure to stay tuned for your favorite game show..."Drawing Molecules for Laundry Money." Now, here's your host Rick Slick! *(APPLAUSE sign raised from behind set)*

RICK: Hey everybody, get ready to play the game that lets contestants use their knowledge of chemistry AND their artistic talent to win big cash prizes. Today our contestant is Ester Bond. *(Enter ESTER BOND, carrying easel on stage, wearing a housecoat and curlers)* Ester is trying to win our big prize of one million wash-and-wear cycles by drawing a molecule in under 30 seconds. Are you ready Ester?

ESTER: Sure am Rick!

RICK: OK, here goes! The molecule you must draw *(Looks at card in hand)*....soap!

ESTER: Oh, that's easy Rick! *(Starts to draw, RICK watches with fake smile)* You see, the soap molecule could actually be compared to a ha ha...lollipop, Rich, and we have a chain or ha, ha, a necklace of lollipops, each with a water-liking or hydrophilic group of atoms here, and a water-repelling, grease-attracting group here...

hydrophilic part   hydrophobic part of molecule
(attracts water)   (repels water, attracts grease)

chain of soap molecules

RICK: *(Very excited)* That's RIGHT, Ester! You're our new cham...*(Applause sign)*

ESTER: *(Using Rick to illustrate)* Now, the soap molecules are able to cut through the water's surface tension, which is sort of like the water's skin. This allows the water to flow more wetly into the areas where there's dirt. Then, the soap molecule grabs onto the grease molecule with one side and the water molecule with the other. Soap pulls the sticky grease away from the dirt particles so when the whole thing is scrubbed or agitated, the water washes away the dirt. *(Points to agitator)* Now dirt...

RICK: *(Fast losing enthusiasm)* Thank you Ester, that was...

ESTER: As studies have shown, the dirt, in every 100 pounds of domestic washing...

RICK: *(Angry)* Fine Ester. Thanks. *(Pushes ESTER off left)* Tune in tomorrow folks to "Drawing Molecules for Laundry Money." *(Exits with easel, changes back to ANNOUNCER)*

ESTER: *(Jumps back on stage from behind set)*...consists of: point nine pounds of protein-free organic matter, point three pounds of proteins, that is, particles of skin, hairs... Point one-five pounds of fatty acids from sweat and greasy excretions, as well as sand, dust, and other... *(Pulled offstage)*

ANNOUNCER: *(Theme music)* We return you now to "As the Soap Churns," the soap opera that asks the quintessential question: can sweet Saponia Handlebar find happiness in the arms of gorgeous Walter Waters, or will she be drawn inexorably into the slimy embrace of Al B. Grease? As we rejoin our program Saponia's kindly Aunt Bubbles, a noted Bubble-ologist, has just returned home.

SCENE II

Enter AUNT BUBBLES, stage left. She begins busying herself with bubble cart, whistling or humming the show's theme music.

AUNT BUBBLES: Now where did I put that glycerin? Ah...here it is...

SAPONIA: *(Enters)* Aunt Bubbles. Oh, thank goodness you're home. I've got to talk with you.

AUNT BUBBLES: Well, of course, my sweet Saponia. Didn't I see Walter Waters leaving just now?

SAPONIA: Yes, he was here. He wanted me to go to the Cleanspot with him.

AUNT BUBBLES: Yes, he's so level-headed. Now dear, what's on your mind?

SAPONIA: That's just it, my mind. I feel like I'm going crazy, like I'm two different people. One part of me is really attracted to Walter Waters...But lately another part of me seems drawn to someone completely different. I just want to grab him and carry him off, if you know what I mean. I guess I can tell you his name...it's Al B. Grease.

AUNT BUBBLES: *(Shuddering)* Grease! I don't think I've met him. What does he do?

SAPONIA: Uh, he works at the gas station and he's a rap artist. *(AUNT BUBBLES cringes)* He's very well known down at the Lint Trap. Maybe you've heard his latest—"My name is Grease and I can rap, if ya don't like my song, better shut your trap."

AUNT BUBBLES: Charming *(Polite to Saponia)*, Charming *(Disgusted to audience)*.

SAPONIA: *(Upset)* Part of me really likes Walter, but part of me is, like, repulsed by him. I'm not sure why. And part of me knows better than to become involved with Al B., but I'm so attracted to him I can't help it.

AUNT BUBBLES: There, there, dear, try to calm down for a minute and listen to me. I've been through a few cycles in my time, and, the way I see it, it all comes down to chemistry.

SAPONIA: Chemistry? But this is my life we're talking about!

AUNT BUBBLES: Ah yes, without chemistry life itself would be impossible! Saponia, I didn't want to be the one to have to tell you this, but the reason you feel torn in two is because you're.......HYDROPHILIC! *(Dramatic chord)*

SAPONIA: Oh! *(Shocked)* Is it true? Is it really true? Am I really Hydrophilic!

AUNT BUBBLES: Yes, Saponia, but that's only half of it. You're also....

SAPONIA: Yes, yes...

AUNT BUBBLES: HYDROPHOBIC!!!! *(Dramatic chord, SAPONIA gasps, they freeze)*

ADVERTISEMENT #3 *(SOAPRAH) (WALTER)*

ANNOUNCER: Are you secretly addicted to mud pies? How do you cope with surface tension? We'll explore hydrophobia and hydrophilia on the next....Soaprah Cling-free show! Immediately following People Are Washing! And now, back to our show!

(AUNT BUBBLES and SAPONIA unfreeze after Announcer finishes)

SAPONIA: I'm Hydrophilic and Hydrophobic. Why does everything have to be so complicated? Why did this have to happen to me? Oh no, oh no! *(To herself)* I hardly know what it all means. In fact, I don't know what it means! *(To Bubbles)* What does it mean?

AUNT BUBBLES: Now Saponia, don't get all worked up into a lather.... *(Plays with bubble apparatus)*

SAPONIA: OK, think. Hydro means water, and philic means loving or liking, so hydrophilic means...

AUNT BUBBLES: That part of you likes and is very attracted to water...

SAPONIA: *(Pondering)* Hydrophilic....

AUNT BUBBLES: But part of you is disgusted and repelled by water. That part of you is Hydrophobic!!!!

SAPONIA: Hydrophobic....hating water. But why me? Why me?

AUNT BUBBLES: Because you are a member of the soap family.

SAPONIA: Well, I know that. My name comes from the word "saponification," which is the chemical reaction that takes place when soap is made.

AUNT BUBBLES: *(Brings tray to SAPONIA to hold. On it are three containers: one marked "BASE," one marked "FATTY ACID," and one into which contents of other two are poured.)* Absolutely correct. When a fat or fatty acid is heated with a base, *(Withdraws tiny bar of soap, sound effect "DING," applause sign goes up from backstage)* soap is made, and that's called saponification.

SAPONIA: But, Aunt Bubbles, why do I find Al B. Grease so attractive?

AUNT BUBBLES: Because the part of you that hates water, the Hydrophobic part, is also very strongly attracted to grease. In fact, you two are chemically related. I'm afraid you just can't help yourself.

SAPONIA: You mean because I'm a soap?

AUNT BUBBLES: Saponia, dear. This is so very upsetting for you. Why don't you and I go out for some candy-coated water chestnuts at the Clean Spot? I could use a treat right now.

SAPONIA: Okay, Aunt Bubbles. I'd like that. I'll go get my coat.

AUNT BUBBLES: Goody! *(Exit SAPONIA and AUNT BUBBLES stage left)*

ANNOUNCER: *(Music)* We'll return to "As the Soap Churns" in just a moment, but first a word about an upcoming program you won't want to miss....*(Music off)*

ADVERTISEMENT #4 *(DR. TALLOW)*

ANNOUNCER: Later tonight on Sudsy Mystery Terror Theater, the chilling tale of "Dr. Tallow and Mr. Tyde." *(Minor chord)*

(ACTOR, using a coffee-sized can labeled "CAUSTIC SODA" on one side, and "GREASE" on the other, pantomimes the transformation of Dr. Tallow as Announcer describes, or Announcer does entire skit, as other actor screams offstage at appropriate spots.)

ANNOUNCER: Dr. Beef Tallow was a mild-mannered fatty acid until one day he was exposed to the mysterious, base substance—— Caustic Soda! *(Actor as Dr. Tallow spills contents of can labelled caustic soda on himself)* This creepy chemical transformed the good doctor into Mr. Tyde, a crazed detergent with an insatiable lust for...grease! *(Thunder clap and scream)*....that's tonight on Sudsy Mystery Terror Theater—a shocking tale of split chemicality—"Dr. Tallow and Mr.

Tyde." *(TALLOW exits. Music)* We return now to the next episode of "As the Soap Churns," where Saponia, in her valiant quest for truth, love, and the chemistry of soap, is still spinning from her Aunt Bubbles' revelations. As Saponia gets ready to go out with Aunt Bubbles, suddenly Walter arrives on the scene....*(Music off)*

SCENE III

WALTER: *(Jumps in)* Where's Saponia? I've got to talk with her.

AUNT BUBBLES: *(From behind stage, only head and torso lean out with Aunt Bubbles' costume held in front to hide Al B. costume)* She's getting ready to go out...to the Clean Spot with me. *(As WALTER moves to find Saponia stage right, AUNT BUBBLES stops him.)* I'll go tell her you're here. *(Exit AUNT BUBBLES stage right)*

WALTER: *(Looks away discreetly)* Thank you, Auntie Bubbles!

(WALTER mutters to himself "charming woman, etc." while he waits. Enter AL B. GREASE.)

AL B.: Well, if it ain't the big drip himself!

WALTER: *(Very tense)* Now listen, you keep your filthy self away from Saponia! *(Slips)*

AL B.: *(Shakes his head, goes over to him)* You OK? Can I help you up?

WALTER: *(Surly)* I can get up by myself, thank you. *(Slips again)* Just keep your dirty hands to yourself! When's the last time you washed?

AL B.: Just tryin' to help. Soap can be slippery stuff.

WALTER: I hardly need you to tell me that!

AL B.: Hey man, you're all wet! I sure don't know what Saponia sees in you...

WALTER: The feeling's mutual, I'm sure...how she could look twice at a sleazeball like you?

AL B.: I warn you, I've got a rhyme degree from Grease University...

WALTER: I trust you will abide by the Marquis of Cleansberry poetic rules...

(The two engage in a word duel, with physical action representing their chemical relationship, i.e., Walter seems unable to get close to Al B., and is repelled by an invisible force, while Al B. is always higher than Walter, in control, unable to be budged, etc. The physical action should not be a fight, not violent or physically combative, but more like magnetic repulsion, facing off, a verbal sparring match. It can increase in volume by the end, but should build slowly and put emphasis on the words and rhymes.)

AL B.: By any rules or any name, Grease is bound to win this game...

WALTER: OK then, you asked for it— I'm water, you're goo, everything you say washes off me and sticks on you!

AL B.: Yeh, well, Grease floats on water, that'll never stop
So no matter what you do, I come out on top! *(On stool)*

WALTER: Hmm...this feels sort of like an invisible shield *(Mimes)*
But I'll turn up the flow and you'll have to yield.

AL B.: Waltie, let's face it, you can't break my defense
You're too tense on the surface and I'm less dense.

WALTER: For all your dirt you're rather elusive
And on top of that you're quite obtrusive!

AL B.: I can float like a butterfly, sting like a bee
My repulsiveness brings me victory!

WALTER and AL B.: *(Face to face, yelling)*
    I'm rubber, you're goo
    Grease floats on water
    I'm rubber, you're goo
    Grease floats on water *(etc)*.

SAPONIA: *(Enters)* What's going on here? *(Both men are at fever pitch)* Stop all this shouting right now. STOP!!! *(They freeze. SAPONIA goes*

into very fast rap. She is beginning to realize her power) Now check this out—
    All ya need to grab grease is saponification
    Provided you have some water flotation
    Then you just add some agi-vibration
    And you'll be engaged in cleanification
    Two-way attraction, liquefaction
    A chain reaction of cleansing action
    For loads and loads of washifaction....

AL B.: Hey Saponia, that was great!

WALTER: I say Saponia, you do have a fluid way with words....

SAPONIA: Now why don't you two just go outside and try to get to know each other better. I've got important matters to discuss with Aunt Bubbles. *(THEY exit, WALTER turns off bubble machine)* Now I wonder what happened to Aunt Bubbles? She's always popping in and popping out. *(Putters with bubble machine)* Aunt Bubbles!? Aunt Bubbles?!

AUNT BUBBLES: *(Changing offstage)* I'll be with you in a minute dear, I'm just taking a bubble bath....

SAPONIA: Take your time! Oh, look at this mess! *(Tries to clean up. Enter AUNT BUBBLES from stage left, is shocked by the mess)* Aunt Bubbles, I'm sorry about this big mess. It's all my fault.

AUNT BUBBLES: No, dear. You know what they say, "oil and water do not mix."

SAPONIA: Oh, Aunt Bubbles, what am I going to do? Walter and Al B. are so different from one another and I'm so different from either of them...

AUNT BUBBLES: Well, you know dear, opposites often attract. Why when your parents first met they were very different.

SAPONIA: Really?

AUNT BUBBLES: Well you know your mother, my sister Olive,

was a gentle, fatty acid who never caused any friction. On the other hand, your father, HyDrox, was a base young fellow with a caustic disposition. When they met it was reaction at first attraction...soon they were engulfed in a burning cauldron of emotion.

SAPONIA: My parents?

AUNT BUBBLES: I know it's hard to believe dear...but it's true. Like other fatty acids and bases who fall in tub with each other, your parents dedicated themselves to clean living and fighting grime when they entered into sanctified saponification.

SAPONIA: And that's how I was born!

AUNT BUBBLES: Yes, you came along and swept away any remaining static cling in their lives. You brought sunshine and light. You were given that necklace when you were born, as a beautiful symbol of your heritage, a reminder of your true destiny...

SAPONIA: *(Proudly)* It represents a chain of soap molecules, and...

AUNT BUBBLES: Yes, it shows how your parents' two different natures combined to create something completely different.

SAPONIA: I get it! Mama was a fatty acid, and Al B. is a grease, and fatty acids and grease are related...maybe that explains my attraction to him...

AUNT BUBBLES: What you've discovered dear, is that when you encounter water or grease...your molecular structure is attracted to *(Builds suspense)* first one, then the other, then one, then the other, and then....

SAPONIA: Yes, yes? Which one should I choose?

AUNT BUBBLES: I'm sorry Saponia, I can't answer that for you, you'll have to find your own way through the sudsing tide...this above all, to thine own soap be true...

SAPONIA: Oh Aunt Bubbles, don't leave me hanging, there's so much changing and rearranging....

AUNT BUBBLES: Well, when you come right down to it, Saponia, that's what chemistry is really all about—CHANGES! *(Siren sound)*

ALL CHARACTERS: *(ACTORS should state clearly that this is a "Washquake")* Oh no! Oh no!! Washquake!!!! Washquake!!!! *(Looking up)* The lid is opening...here comes the Detergent! *(Styrofoam is dumped from huge soap box poised over set)* It'll all come out in the wash!!!!!!!!!!!!!!!! It'll all come out in the wash!!!!!!

(ALL characters run madly around the stage.)

SAPONIA: Al B.! Where are you Al B.!??? Oh, no, I can't see him anywhere—I must find him! Al B! Al B! *(ALL exit stage left, bubble cart taken off, siren is turned off, rock music comes up.)*

ADVERTISEMENT #5 (ELVIS) (WALTER & SAPONIA)

ANNOUNCER: New from Wash and Tell! The greatest hits of the greatest legend of all time! Elvis Permanent Pressley: the King of Wash and Wear!

(Elvis look-alike comes on stage and waves to audience.)

ELVIS: *(Sung to tune of "All Shook Up." Music heavy on drums)*

> Well my pants are pressed
> And my shirt is neat I can't seem to sing
> Till I wash my feet
>
> I'm in suds...suds
> Uh-huh, uh-huh, ya-ya ya
> I'm all washed up!

ANNOUNCER: Act now and receive a free lollipop necklace as a special gift! Our toll-free operators are standing by, ready to take your orders for the greatest hits of Elvis Permanent Pressley, the King of Wash & Wear! *(Musical flourish)*

We return you now to our exciting real-life drama. *(Music)* As you recall, when the Big Washquake came, Al B. was nowhere to be seen. *(Enter AL B.)*

Then everyone discovered that poor Al B. had been caught, imprisoned by threads and fibers, in the Lint Trap. Desperately struggling to break free, Al B. only seems to further glue his globules to the sticking point. Meanwhile, deep within the churning tub, millions of molecules watch as the tense drama unfolds. Could this be his final cycle? Let's rejoin our suds saga and find out...

SCENE IV

At the Lint Trap. AL B. is seen on stage, far stage right...as if buried or enmeshed in a prison of fibers/fabric...he is struggling to break free.

AL B.: *(Pushing hand up)* If I could only unravel this thread...but this elastic fiber is pinning down my legs. I don't know how much longer I can keep my grip. I feel like I'm hanging by a thread! HELP!!!!!!

(WALTER & SAPONIA enter stage left, hear AL B.'s cries)

WALTER: *(To audience)* This looks like a real thread-hanger! No wonder they call it the Lint Trap!

AL B.: Help!

SAPONIA: Hang on Al B., help is on its way.

AL B.: Help!

WALTER: *(To SAPONIA, who's reaching, stretching, trying to tunnel or extend through the imaginary rubble)* You can't go in there Saponia, it's too dangerous!

AL B: M'aidez! M'aidez!

SAPONIA: I must save him, and Walter—you must help me!

AL B.: Socorro!

WALTER: Why me? I mean I just never could get close to him. Something about him just rub-a-dub-dubs me the wrong way.

AL B.: Help!

SAPONIA: *(Massages Walter's shoulders)* C'mon Walter, get rid of all that surface tension. We'll never get in close enough to Al B. unless you loosen up.

AL B.: Help!

WALTER: *(Feeling the effects)* For you Saponia, I'll flow anywhere.

SAPONIA: *(Sings a la Whitney Houston)* Just give me one moment in grime when I'm racing with my destiny...

AL B.: Help!

WALTER: *(To audience, as SAPONIA leads, firmly holding Walter's hand, wiggles in, grabs hold of AL B.'s hand with her other hand, they pull him out)* Please note the excellent example of how a soap molecule latches on firmly to both a water molecule and a grease molecule. Then when we are shaken up or scrubbed *(Actions mimic all of this)* the grease is pulled out by the soap...

SAPONIA: And the soap is pulled out by the water...pull, Walter, pull!

WALTER: I'm pulling, Schnookums....

AL B.: *(Gasping, makes popping sound as HE is pulled out)* I'm saved!

SAPONIA: OK everybody, we're coming out. Walter, be sure to wash away those dirt particles now that we've dislodged Al B. *(All three come to center stage, holding hands, to sing and dance the finale.)*

    Hey we got the grease
    The grease is free
    Pulled him hydrophilically

    Get a little soap
    And you will see
    You'll be as clean as me

    Glad you got me out
    At last I'm free
    Pulled me hydrophobically

> When we pull together
> What's it mean
> The chemistry of clean.

ANNOUNCER: *(Over musical bridge)* And that concludes another stirring episode. Will our three stalwart molecules be swept down the drain? Tune in next week, same soap tub, same soap station, for "As The Soap Churns." *(Runs back, song continues)*

> We're hoping now at last
> That you have learned
> That's the way
> The old soap churns
> When we pull together
> It's a fact
> Our molecules attract! *(I mean to tell ya)*
>
> Our molecules attract! *(Believe me baby)*
>
> Our molecules attra-a-a-a-ct!

(Music up for final stanza, ACTORS bow and exit during applause, WALTER takes longer, looks around, realizes slapstick-style that he's on stage alone, then exits.)

THE END

WONDROUS VISIONS: A VISIT WITH LEONARDO DA VINCI

BY **Dick Goldberg**

5

© The Franklin Institute, 1986

Self-portrait of Leonardo da Vinci (1452-1519).

PLAYWRIGHT'S NOTES

"Wondrous Visions" was researched by Sheila Garred, then a museum educator at the Franklin Institute and now education coordinator at the Baltimore Museum of Industry in Maryland. It was written by Dick Goldberg, a local playwright with numerous theater and television scripts to his credit, and directed by Andy Lichtenberg, then Director of the Walnut Street Theater School.

The process began with the preparation of a brief concept outline by Sheila Garred. This contained three objectives and notes on the content which needed to be conveyed. It was decided that the script should be geared to a fifth-grade reading level. Next, a more fleshed-out position piece was completed. Having done considerable reading on and thinking about the subject matter, Ms. Garred was able to give rather developed guidelines to the playwright before he began his work. She also provided him with copies of Leonardo's drawings, a timeline of his work, pictures of the castle where he lived at the end of his life and other background material. Suggestions were made for science demonstrations which would be both illustrative of Leonardo's work and able to be built by staff members in the Museum's tech shop.

The playwright's job was then to pare down some of the content and write the script. An interesting dynamic occurred between Ms. Garred, who saw the program from an educational perspective, and Mr. Goldberg, who approached the project as a piece of drama. Eventually, both realized that (a) drama is not teaching or it would be a demonstration and (b) a museum is different from a theater. At one point, Ms. Garred described how Leonardo was like a "monkey in a zoo" in his later years, trotted out by King Francis to perform for his guests. From this, Mr. Goldberg came up with the idea of having Leonardo answer pretend questions from visitors to his bottega. Throughout this process, the playwright looked for the inherent drama in the material he was given to work with.

It should be noted that several of the demonstration ideas originally presented to the playwright were never produced, for a number of reasons. A plan to use exhibit models too delicate to be handled by visitors never materialized. A famous optical experiment was eliminated because it involved using real fire on stage. Some demonstrations would not fit the dramatic flow of the piece. Others were selected, but either never made it off the drawing board or failed during construction. A few were simply not able to be demonstrated by actors untrained in the "art" of performing science experi-

ments for the public.
   The playwright produced drafts of the script, which were then reviewed by Ms. Garred, Mr. Lichtenberg, and other Franklin Institute staff members involved with the project. Eventually, what began as "Leonardo da Vinci: A Mind's Eye" became "Wondrous Visions: A Visit with Leonardo da Vinci."

PRODUCTION HISTORY AND NOTES

   In the summer of 1986, The Franklin Institute hosted "Leonardo da Vinci: Genius at Work," an exhibit developed by the IBM Corporation with the help of scientists, engineers and craftsmen from around the world. The exhibit transformed drawings from Leonardo's famous notebooks into three-dimensional working models—among them his famous parachute, helicopter and spring-driven car. In keeping with his Renaissance spirit, the Museum featured a variety of summer programs and events to enhance the exhibit.
   The centerpiece of this programming was "Wondrous Visions: A Visit with Leonardo da Vinci." This 25-minute dramatic presentation, featuring a single actor, was set in the master's workshop (or bottega) at the Castle of King Francis of France. The play portrays Leonardo as an old and eccentric genius who reminisces about his life as artist, inventor, and scientist.
   "Wondrous Visions" was presented daily at 11:30 a.m. (except Sundays), 1:30 and 3:30 p.m. from July through August, for a total of 192 times to more than 23,000 visitors. A stage was built in the William Penn Gallery (the Museum's special exhibits hall), with bleacher seating for approximately 120 visitors.
   It was possible to turn lights off in the rest of the exhibit while bringing lights up on the stage for the performance. Drapes on either side of the bleachers, which faced away from the exhibit at the far end of the gallery, provided a slight visual barrier between the two areas. The original notion was simply to discourage visitors from using exhibit devices while the play was in progress; it was soon obvious that any noise was too much of a distraction and the exhibit was essentially closed during performances. The actor did not use a microphone.
   A background panel was designed and built by Quinlan Studios, a Philadelphia-area scene shop. This panel was mounted at the rear of two carpeted platforms which served as the stage. The set consisted of a large table and several props built especially for the

program. (Unfortunately, The Franklin Institute no longer has these props, although the person who built them is still an occasional employee at the Institute.) A suitable costume was rented for the run of the play from Pierre's, a professional costume shop serving the theater community.

Andy Lichtenberg and Sheila Garred worked with a casting agency to locate prospective actors to audition for the role of Leonardo. In addition, Mr. Lichtenberg was able to recruit a pool of candidates from his contacts at the Walnut Street Theater, one of Philadelphia's best-known theater companies. Eventually, some 30 people were auditioned and two were selected to perform, with each given equal billing. Because of this arrangement, only one performance was cancelled during the two month period.

The rehearsal period lasted three-and-a-half weeks, with the first two weeks at the Walnut Street Theater and final rehearsals at The Franklin Institute. Once the play opened, the Director made only occasional visits, with Sheila Garred assuming production responsibilities for the play. A staff person was always assigned to the area to assist with crowd control and technical needs. A dressing room area, complete with cot and make-up table, was set up nearby to allow the actor to prepare for performances and rest in between them.

Total cost for the play was $17,500. This broke down as follows:

Research	$ 1,000
Playwright	1,200
Director	1,500
Actors	7,500
Casting	300
Set	2,000
Props	1,500
Costumes/Make-up	1,000
Videotape Production	1,500

As a point of reference, the development of "Air, Wings, and Flying Things," a science show which also ran during this time period in the museum's 320-seat auditorium, cost $3,700. This program was developed and presented completely by in-house staff. A survey was developed and carried out which looked at the audiences' response to both the exhibit and the performance.

103

MARKETING

A brochure highlighting all of the components of the da Vinci program was distributed throughout the city and was used primarily to attract summer tourists. Press releases were sent out about the play, planetarium show, and opening weekend. A general release on all of the da Vinci-related programs was also prepared. Paid radio advertising was used to promote the Renaissance Fair.

We received TV news coverage on the opening weekend as well as a feature article in the June 27th Weekend section of the Philadelphia Inquirer. Press clippings were received from many local papers in the area and a "91 Report" story on WHYY-FM on the da Vinci program was featured in late August. Two Captain Noah programs also featured segments on the da Vinci program.

ATTENDANCE

June 28 - August 28/	1986	1985	1984
Individuals	89,083	85,536	68,982
Groups	16,357	17,828	13,316
Total	105,440	103,364	107,510

ANALYSIS

In order to assist in the assessment of this program, questionnaires were developed and six hundred visitors were surveyed on eight different days to determine why they came to the museum, what they like and disliked about their visit, and other demographic characteristics. One questionnaire was administered to visitors as they entered the building, another was used to survey visitors as they left the museum.

Additionally, one hundred and fifty-three visitors were surveyed immediately following the "Wondrous Visions" play on different days throughout the summer in order to find out their reaction to this type of program.

SUMMARY OF "WONDROUS VISIONS" SURVEY
91% of the respondents found the play very easy to understand
84% rated the play highly educational
87% rated the play highly entertaining
93% said that seeing the performance made their visit to the museum more enjoyable
98% indicated that they would recommend the performance to their friends.
50% said that they would have been willing to pay to see the performance
79% indicated that the performance caused them to become more interested in the exhibit

Although most of the results were highly positive, low marks were received for seating and acoustics. Thirty-one % of the people indicated that the seating was inadequate and 24% of those polled were displeased with the acoustics. Seating was available for approximately 120 visitors and the average attendance per show was approximately 125 visitors, indicating that standing room only was the norm. Extraneous noise during the play was frequently a problem.

Some trends revealed by the study include: 25 percent of the people visiting the museum were from outside the three-state area. This compares with 16 percent during the fall of 1984. The size of the party seems to have changed also. Sixty-eight percent of the people visiting this summer attended in a group of three or more people versus 57 percent in the fall of 1984.

Significantly more people had heard advertising about the Franklin Institute before coming this summer, compared to the fall of 1984 (38 percent vs. 28 percent). This is particularly impressive since nearly all of the surveys in 1984 were administered immediately following a paid advertising campaign, whereas only two of the eight interview days this summer followed paid advertising.

Seventy-six percent of the visitors surveyed indicated that they were college graduates versus 56 percent in 1984 and 17 percent nationally. In terms of the summer program, the results seemed very positive: The two programs that people most frequently mentioned as best liked were the "Wondrous Visions" play and "Renaissance Skies" planetarium show. Both in terms of quality and appropriateness, this survey seems to indicate that the da Vinci summer program was successful. Additionally, assuming that these results are representative of our summer audience—14 percent of our visitors came to the museum primarily because of the da Vinci program—this translates into nearly 15,000 visitors. It seems to suggest that the program was financially responsible as well.

Packaging our summer program thematically seems to have had a positive impact on both the visitor experience and overall attendance.

PRODUCTION RIGHTS

The Franklin Institute owns the rights to the production of "Wondrous Visions." Because the script was commissioned, the museum receives a $300 fee each time the play is produced for up to a three-month period. A $25 fee is charged for review of the script and the accompanying videotape which was made of an actual performance. All sets and props would need to be constructed by the producing organization unless an additional arrangement were made with The Franklin Institute (and this would be costly). To date, the play has been produced about six times, but only once by another museum, the Museum of Scientific Discovery in Harrisburg, Pennsylvania, where the original production was lent for the museum's opening weekend of the *Leonardo da Vinci* exhibition.

For further information on this and other theater presentations at The Franklin Institute, please contact Sarah Orleans, Manager of Special Programs, The Franklin Institute, 20th and the Parkway, Philadelphia, PA 19103; 215/448-1184.

WONDROUS VISIONS: A VISIT WITH LEONARDO DA VINCI

(LEONARDO'S bottega at Castle Amboise. Before the house lights dim and the lights on the bottega come up, we hear prerecorded the general hubbub of an excited crowd, and then above the noise of the crowd, a MAN'S VOICE: "Hurry—it's time! Leonardo is about to speak!" Then a WOMAN'S VOICE: "He's the greatest human being in captivity—hah!" SECOND MAN'S VOICE: "I heard he was very interesting." Then a SECOND WOMAN'S VOICE: "Quiet! Here he comes!" The CROWD quiets down. Lights down on the house, up on the set; music—a Renaissance processional;

LEONARDO enters and studies the audience, then sighs a few times as if he were making interesting discoveries about various members of the audience. Music out.)

LEONARDO: Welcome to my *bottega*, my workshop. King Francis told me I would have more visitors today. He likes to show me off. But the way he describes me to people like you who come to visit him—I ask you, would you like being called Leonardo the Divine? Please don't misunderstand—I did appreciate his invitation last year to come to France, to live here at Castle Amboise, and be the "first painter and engineer to the King"... but still to be referred to as "the greatest human being in captivity"—as I heard one of you do—well, it can make one feel—how shall I say it? A little unsettled.... Ah, but you're not here to listen to the complaints of an old man, are you? You're here to ask questions. So.... *(Calls on someone in the audience.)* Yes? *(Pretends to listen to the question)* How old am I? *(With a touch of exasperation)* Very well—today, in the year of our Lord, 1517—sixty-five... If you wouldn't mind, I think I might prefer—how shall I say it?...more intelligent questions.

(Another question)

What was my life like as a young man? Now, you have asked something that is both a happy and a sad question for me. Happy because it makes me remember... and sad, because I will never live anything like those days again.... I was born about twenty miles from Florence—that, as I am sure you know, is in Italy. In a little town called Vinci; hence, when I am not being called "the greatest human being in—" et cetera, I am known simply as Leonardo da Vinci.... When I was 16, my family moved to Florence, where I became an artist's apprentice. That town was filled with life! As was I— life, and the need to know—everything! The other young men there—they wore long grey and black robes. But I—I went about in crimson and blue and silver, which set off my long, curling hair—It was red then... *(Laughs)*

I just remembered something I used to enjoy doing so much in the marketplace there in Florence—setting the birds free from their cages—yes, that's what I did! I *loved* watching the birds fly—I still do! I hold my breath—it is so beautiful! Actually, they sort of leap— did you know that? They beat their wings down to make a wave of air...*(Demonstrates)* The air strikes at the bird's breast from below...which makes the bird leap upward. How did I learn this? Simply from *closely* observing birds in flight... I once built a flying machine—wings for a man...*(Gestures toward model of this invention)* but it didn't work...

(Another question)

If people were stronger, would they be able to fly? *(Delighted with the question)* Very good. If we had more strength in our arms, it's possible we might be able to create a wave of air powerful enough to support us. The study of the human body—its strength, its beauty, and how it works—that has fascinated me all my life—and has also got me in trouble....uh... never mind about that. I have designed hundreds and hundreds of inventions and machines—mostly I've sketched them here in my notebooks—where I always write backwards. See! *(Takes a volume from the table and shows a page with a design for an invention "Leonardo" is written backwards in capital letters. Leafs through the volume to show the audience the various designs HE refers to)* Designs for other kinds of flying machines... rotisseries—you know rotisseries? For roasting meat! Water pumps...automobiles. When I see an idea in my mind's eye, I have to get it down on paper in one of these books! But there is nothing more beautiful and complex than the human body.

Do you know how the muscles work? I will tell you: when you want to move an object—this table, for instance... *(Starts to pull the table)* your muscles don't just pull it—they work against each other—and that's what makes the table move. *(Strains and the table moves)* This I discovered in my studies of anatomy. The flight of birds... to the movements of humans—it's really all of one piece. And my study of anatomy—it frequently led me to—geometry! Believe me, if you look closely enough, you can see beauty everywhere! Let the alchemists try to change everything into gold—which, of course, they will never be able to do—there is knowledge worth far more than gold to be had by looking closely at the beauty and balance *already there in nature*. I will show you—*I will show you that beauty within yourself!* A volunteer perhaps? *(Scans the audience before carefully choosing)* You—you would be fine! *(Gestures to a member of the audience)* Stand—stand over there please. *(Indicates a platform)*

Now, please place your feet apart so that your height is reduced about one/fourteenth... Yes, I know—who is used to thinking about such an unusual fraction? But there is beauty in numbers. One/fourteenth—here, let me help you. *(Judges 1/14 of the volunteer's height and keeps gesturing for volunteer to move his/her feet to achieve this posture)* Good... good... a little more... now, up just the tiniest amount—fine. Now, raise your arms so that your fingertips are level with the top of your head. You will please now indicate where your navel is. Why do all of King Francis' friends laugh when I say that word? Very well, now do any of you know what this measuring device is called? *(Gets a huge compass)* Right, a compass! In my life I have designed many different ones—drawing circles, ellipses, making reductions. This one is for—a circle, a large circle! Now, let us see what happens, when we use the navel as the center of the body, and the distance to the fingertips as a radius... *(Draws in the air)* This looks familiar? Perhaps you have seen somewhere a drawing of mine similar to this. You will please now direct your attention to the triangle formed by the legs—it is a perfect equilateral one—three beautiful lines of equal length! Anatomy—geometry—art! *(Directs the volunteer to return to his/her seat)* Thank you.

(Another question)

How did my studies of the human body get me in trouble? Not easily diverted, are you? *(Thinks about whether to answer this question)* Very well. Five years ago, when I was living and working in Rome, I was secretly accused—I'm fairly sure it was by one of my former students—I was secretly accused of—dissecting corpses. The accusation was... true. The Pope forbade me to continue; I stopped. What my student, and God forgive me for saying so, the Pope did not understand, is that to study anatomy, as in the study of flight or motion or geometry or anything else—one needs to look closely. Only then, can one hope to see—really see—nature's incredible beauty. Within the body, there is not only such beauty but also a marvelous sense of balance! That balance even affects how we move. Imagine, if you will, a line that cuts you right across the middle. *(Demonstrates)* In order to rise from a sitting position to a standing one, you must thrust everything above that line—the upper half of your body—forward—that is, throw more weight in the direction you want to go than you do in the opposite direction. I will prove this to you! All of you, lean back and without pushing with your arms, try to stand up! Now lean forward—the direction in which you want to go—and try to stand! You all did that very well—I knew from the moment I first saw you that you could stand. *(Gestures for them to sit)*

(Another question)

What is my definition of science? I like that question! I have a fairly far-reaching, wide-ranging notion of what science is. Science, I believe, is the knowledge of things past, present, and possible. And I think we study science because it is the natural desire of good men to know about their world. As a scientist, I really have but one objective, one goal: to *search for inner causes*. To think about what I have seen. To draw a picture of it—my notebooks are filled with pictures about both things I have seen and things I have imagined! And what do I do after I have drawn my picture? Consider the possibilities. No, I didn't mean that you should *consider the possibilities* of what I could do—I mean, that's what I do—consider the possibilities of what I have imagined or drawn... or merely pondered.

Here, let me show you! *(Pulls down blade embedded in block of wood, so that it vibrates)* How many blades do you see? *(As it comes to rest)* How many now? We know it is not many blades—so what must we conclude? That the eye is not quick enough. *You must look closely... and consider the possibilities.* Which can mean you should look at something when it is in motion. *(Pushes the blade so that it again begins vibrating)* For the eye can play many a trick. I shall show you! We shall take a closer look... and find out what is really happening! Another volunteer please! *(Selects one)* You! And another! *(Selects a second volunteer)* You... Stand in front of the mirror, both of you, please. You on the right, touch the mirror where you see your neighbor's left eye reflected. You on the left, whose eye did (s)he touch? *(Audience member on left should respond something along the lines of, "He looked like (s)he was touching his/her own eye")* Let's try it again. You, on the left, touch the mirror where you see your neighbor's right eye reflected. You on the right now, whose eye did (s)he touch? *(Audience member on right should respond similarly. LEONARDO now directs the volunteers to their seats)* Thank you. *(Holds a V-shaped piece of glass tubing to the mirror)* They saw what they did because light hits the mirror at this angle and bounces off at the same angle—another trick played on the eye! The great Greek mathematician Euclid discovered that idea... and my experiment proves it—you must get a friend and try it yourself—yes? Experimentation, you see, is another very important part of how I conduct my studies. To tell you the truth, it's also another way in which my work has been different; most other scientists before me simply theorized—had ideas; I call them "speculators." This is what I do: after I suspect a principle or law of nature, I test it, change some of the variables, and measure results.

Do I consider myself more an artist... or a scientist? Another very interesting question. You're a much brighter group than I usually get. *(Thinks)* A... an... a—an artist! But one who is fascinated by natural energy at work—the swirling of water, the growth of plants, the move-ment of faces, the scintillating passage of light. I studied nature—the flight of birds, anatomy, the mechanics and physics of movement, geometry, the wondrous and mysterious play of light. I studied all of these things and more. But ultimately, my purpose was to try to master artistic design.

You like that answer? I'm not sure I do. I confess: sometimes I think I lost interest in art and turned towards science because, quite frankly, my painting or drawing or casting of statues did not always go so well. I will tell you a story. I once was asked to paint a giant fresco—a painting on a wall. The subject was to be a battle. Because I wanted a realistic depiction, I relied on sketches I had made of many battles I had observed at close range, sometimes a little bit too close perhaps, but how can you create a realistic picture unless you have looked closely, yes? I spent months on this fresco, and even devised a special formula for the paint. Would you like to see it? You can't. The wall for the fresco was made of plaster; my "special formula" for the paint eventually dripped right off.

(Takes a moment to see the paint dripping from the wall, then hears another question. Pauses, becomes excited)

Water! I haven't told you anything about my work with water, and these days I'm intrigued by water. From the Greek scientist Heron, I know that water always rises or settles to the same height whenever you pour it into something. *(Demonstrates by pouring colored water into a V-shaped glass tube)* You see! But what of water when it moves, how does it behave then? If I were to apply the same force in pushing down the plungers into each of these vessels... *(Indicates two standing tubes, one tube much wider than the other, each contains a plunger, and water)* which column of water do you think would spout higher? This one? That one? *(Audience responds)* Well, let us see... Please, at the same time and with equal force, remember. *(Does so)* Using equal amounts of water and applying the same amount of pressure, the narrower the vessel, the higher the fountain it creates—an observation we could confirm by my method of experimentation! Closely observing these phenomena and others led me to invent a nautical lock for moving boats from water of a low level to water at a much higher one,

111

and to change the flow of rivers and even waterfalls! Water can be very fascinating, yes?

(Another question)

Did I ever have fun? Isn't this fun? Oh, you mean besides the joy my work and discoveries have given me? Yes! I've done some very silly things in my life—who hasn't?

(Another question, thinking he has avoided the specifics)

What were they? Well- I once glued a very convincing pair of wings to a live lizard and passed it off as a small dragon... *(Mimes doing this)* And on occasion I have been known to inflate the lungs from an ox like giant balloons until they crowded everyone in the room against the walls. Would you call that fun?

(Another question)

In a life filled with achievement, was there ever any disappointment or failure? You mean besides my human wings— *(Gestures toward that invention)* and my fresco that slid off the wall? Sometimes I have felt like asking myself a slightly different question: in a life filled with failure, was there ever any real achievement? A difference of perception, of what the "mind's eye" sees, no? You see the water—I see the air. *(Points to V-tubes)* But to answer your question: sometimes I have felt quite disappointed. *(Hesitates)*

    Do you remember what happened to me five years ago in Rome—the business with...my studies of anatomy. I had *gone* to Rome because I was certain that Cardinal Giuliano, the brother of the Pope, would be helpful to me. During my stay there, the painter Raphael was doing frescoes in the Vatican, that no-talent Michelangelo was ruining the ceiling of the Sistine Chapel...but for Leonardo, they could find no work. All they could find were secret accusations. I was so angry I wanted to scream out at all of them—including the Pope—that they knew nothing, that even some of their dearly held beliefs were idiocy—like their precious notion that the sun revolves around the earth! What nonsense! But given that the punishment for voicing such ideas, which they call heresy, is excommunication and burning at the stake, I decided to keep my... *(realizing he has gone too far)* my theory that possibly it is the planets which revolve around the sun—I decided to keep that "wild notion" to myself.

I ask you if other, lesser talents were being showered with commissions for work and all you were getting were slaps on the wrist and angry fingers shaken in your face, wouldn't you have accepted King Francis' invitation to move once again—and become "first painter and engineer to the king?" *(Beat)* Another move. It has, I think, been quite a vagabond life—Vinci, Florence, Milan, Rome, Amboise.

(Another question)

What is my main interest today? I spend a good bit of my time now imagining how the world might end. Don't be alarmed, I'm not predicting it, but as an old man, I have a right to think about such things, no? The beginning and the end of things, and how you get from birth to death. In a way, that's what I've studied all my life. My studies suggest to me that in oldest times, salt waters entirely occupied and covered the earth, another notion that at present seems to have no other believers. *(Gets one of the Deluge Drawings, but does not show the audience)* But so I believe it was at the beginning-and so I believe it will be at the end! *(Shows the drawing)*. Nature—crumbling rocks and swirling air and *water* have always fascinated me! I have *used my knowledge of those things* to fashion art—art that imagines the ultimate destiny of the elements. *(Beat. Stands looking out the window, as if transfixed. Clock bell sounds)* Ah, the clock I designed to "sound an alarm" is telling me our time together is up. I have more visitors coming at *(Gives actual time for next scheduled performance)*. King Francis likes to keep the "greatest human being in captivity" busy... but now I must rest. *(Starts to exit, then turns back to the audience)* But I will tell you, *this* visit I have enjoyed. You really seemed to want to know, to look closely and learn about the "inner causes." And that is, that is everything.... because it can lead you to ideas, connections, inventions that no one before you ever dreamt existed! Be careful getting up! Throw the weight forward—yes?! *(A gentle laugh, then music—the same Renaissance processional as in the beginning, and LEONARDO exits.)*

THE END

ABOUT ASTC

The Association of Science-Technology Centers (ASTC) is a nonprofit organization of museums and related institutions dedicated to increasing public understanding and appreciation of science and technology.

ASTC and its members recognize the unique potential of science museums to provide informal science education through programs and interactive exhibits. ASTC seeks to improve the operations of science museums, to facilitate communicate among its members, and to help museums broaden and diversify their audiences as well as serve as educational resources for their communities.

ASTC's major services include organizing and circulating hands-on science exhibitions to North American museums; publishing a bimonthly newsletter and other related literature; conducting an annual conference and workshops on various topics; representing science centers with Congress, government agencies, industry, foundations, and other organizations concerned with science education; conducting surveys according to member needs on such topics as salaries, science center operation costs, and programs; and administering a Reciprocal Free Admission Program, in which participating museums waive general admission fees for one another's members.

ASTC currently has more than 350 members representing some 30 countries. Although ASTC members vary in size, scope, and style, all are committed to increasing science literacy.

ASTC is supported by member dues, fees for services, and grants from federal agencies, private foundations, and corporations.